OSCOTT SERIES 1

THE UNSEALED FOUNTAIN

B.C.

THE UNSEALED FOUNTAIN

Essays on the Christian spiritual tradition

Edited with an Introduction

by

The Archbishop of Birmingham

VERITAS

First published 1987 by
Veritas Publications
7-8 Lower Abbey Street
Dublin 1

© Trustees of Saint Mary's College, Oscott, 1987

ISBN 0 86217 243 8

*The Publishers are grateful to the following for permission to reproduce
their copyright material:*
SPCK and Paulist Press, *Athanasius'* The life of Anthony, the
Letter to Marcellinus, trs. Robert Gregg; A. & C. Black and John
Baker Ltd, *John of the Cross, The Living Flame of Love*, trs. David
Lewis; Ignatius Press, *Faith According to John of the Cross*, Karol
Wojtyla, trs. Jordan Aumann; Ave Maria Press, *Healing*, Francis
McNutt; SPCK and Paulist Press, *Showings*, trs. E. Colledge OSA
and J. Walsh SJ; Doubleday & Co. Inc, *The Cloud of Unknowing*,
ed. William Johnston and *The Stairway of Perfection*, Walter Hilton;
Sheed & Ward Ltd, *A Treasury of Russian Spirituality*, ed. G.P.
Fedotov; Darton, Longman & Todd Ltd and Macmillan
Publishing, *Angels and Dirt: An Enquiry into Theology and People*,
John Drury; Burns & Oates Ltd, *On Englishing the Bible*, Ronald
Knox; Faber & Faber Ltd, *St Francis de Sales: Selected Letters*, trs.
E. Stopp, and *The Diary of a Russian Priest*, Alexander Elchaninov,
trs. Helen Iswolsky; The Tablet Publishing Co. Ltd; Geoffrey Bles,
The Great Divorce, A Dream, C.S. Lewis; A.R. Mowbray & Co. Ltd,
The Sayings of the Desert Fathers, trs. Benedicta Ward; A.P. Watt
Ltd, on behalf of The Grail, England and Wm Collins Sons & Co.
Ltd, *The Psalms: A New Translation*; the other Scripture quotations
contained herein are from the Revised Standard Version of the
Bible, copyrighted 1946, 1952, 1971 by the Division of Christian
Education of the National Council of the Churches of Christ in
the USA, and are used by permission.

Cover design: Jim Kilgarriff
Typesetting: Printset & Design Ltd., Dublin
Printed in the Republic of Ireland by Mount Salus Press Ltd.,
Dublin

Foreword

Oscott College was founded near Birmingham in 1794 at a time when students and staff from the English Catholic Colleges abroad were being driven home by the French Revolution. In 1838 it occupied new buildings at Sutton Coldfield, built in the Gothic style, in a move which inaugurated an ambitious new phase of the Catholic Revival in England. St Mary's College, Oscott, is the seminary of the Archdiocese of Birmingham which also has students from many other dioceses in England and Wales.

The *Oscott Series* aims at continuing the role of Oscott as an intellectual and spiritual centre of English Catholicism for close on 200 years. All the contributions contained in this volume, except for No. 10, were first given at an open course of lectures at the College during the winter term of 1983. I am grateful to the Rector and Trustees of the College for accepting my suggestion that they deserve to be published for a wider audience.

+ Maurice

✠ Maurice Couve de Murville
Archbishop of Birmingham

Contents

Contributors

Fr John Berry BA	Assistant Chaplain Cambridge University Catholic Chaplaincy
Miss Judith Champ MA, PhD	Lecturer in Ecclesiastical History at Kings College, London Part-time Lecturer in Ecclesiastical History, Oscott College
Fr Kenneth Collins STL, L SS	Lecturer in Biblical Studies, Oscott College Part-time Lecturer in the Theology Faculty, Birmingham University
Archbishop Maurice Couve de Murville MA, MPhil, STL	Archbishop of Birmingham
W. Jardine Grisbrooke MA	Sometime Lecturer in Liturgy, Oscott College
Fr Austin Hughes SCJ, BD	Part-time Lecturer in Ecclesiastical History, Oscott College
Canon Peter Lawler ✠	Formerly Lecturer in Fundamental Theology, Oscott College Parish Priest Maryvale, Birmingham
Fr Kevin McDonald, BA, STL	Sometime Lecturer in Moral Theology, Oscott College Secretariat for Christian Unity, Rome
Fr David McGough, SR, L SS	Part-time Lecturer in Biblical studies, Oscott College; Parish Priest of Kingstanding, Birmingham
Fr David McLoughlin, STL	Lecturer in Dogmatic Theology, Oscott College
Fr Mervyn Tower, MA, L SS	Lecturer in Biblical Studies, Oscott College

Introduction

The Christian spiritual tradition

What is Christian spirituality? Why the need for spirituality when a Christian has received at Baptism the gift of divine life? Since something as overwhelming as that has occurred, why bother about lesser things? Isn't it like looking at the road map when one can fly an aeroplane?

I suggest that the answer to these questions comes from looking at the limitations of human life on the one hand and the richness of God on the other.

One of the characteristics of human life on earth is that it is not experienced all at once. Time is of the essence; there is no development without it. The normal human being grows through experience, his own and other people's.[1] God is our creator as well as our saviour. He does not abolish our humanity in elevating it to sonship in Christ and pouring out his Spirit upon us. According to the scholastic adage *gratia non tollit naturam sed perfecit*, 'grace does not abolish nature but perfects it'. The educative process which is part of being *man in time* has its parallel in the experience of a Christian.

The New Testament writers give many examples of this as they take in hand those who have had the overwhelming experience of conversion to Christ and Baptism; they guide them so that their Christianity can gradually permeate all aspects of their behaviour and of their personality. So St Paul in his letter to the newly baptised Christians at Rome emphasises the absolute newness of their life in Christ after Baptism (*Romans 6:4*) but this does not prevent him from uttering several pages of moral advice to them (chapters *12-16*) which can be summed up in his phrase: 'do not be conformed to this world but be transformed by the renewal of your minds' (*12:2*) and it is the same in all his letters.

Human limitation explains the need for spirituality in another way; because of the richness of the divine gift no single human being can receive it in its entirety except Christ. He is the fullness of God's revelation to man 'for in him all the fullness of God was pleased to dwell' (*Colossians 1:19*). Every Christian is called to be like Christ but that growth takes place within the community which St Paul likens to the body of Christ where there is complementarity between all the members. As there is variety of gifts in the ministry, so there are many gifts in the growth into Christ. There is no dull uniformity; the sanctity of individuals, the tradition of communities and of spiritual families, are so many ways of reflecting the richness of God's life communicated to man in Jesus Christ, until at the end of history Christ shall deliver the Kingdom, complete at last, to the Father 'that God may be all in all' (*1 Corinthians 15:24-8*). Bearing in mind these two aspects of human limitation and divine richness, a definition of spirituality would run something like this: Christian spirituality is constituted by those attitudes, beliefs and practices which actualise the Gospel in the lives of individuals and groups on their journey to God.

From these general remarks more particular considerations can be made. Firstly, every individual Christian has a spirituality of his own or her own, even if it is not recognised as such. It is made up of what one remembers from religious instruction, quotations from the Bible, bits from the lives of Saints, the attitudes towards religion and towards the Church that we have learnt from our parents, our experience of liturgy, etc. Thus it is revealing to hear about one of the sources of spirituality of St Elizabeth of Hungary in the early thirteenth century when her chronicler writes that she spoke often of the holiest things that she had heard in sermons.[2] These elements are taken up into our personal story and are acted on by our conscious strivings and by our sinfulness too. God's grace is active in all that happens to us but he does not annihilate our individuality. Each person's spirituality is shaped by an individual experience and carried by a particular character. Sometimes this is seen more clearly in the lives of those who are not saints or spiritual writers. Thus Louis XIV, at a time when Communion was rare, used to go to Holy Communion five times a year, wearing the robes of the Order of the Holy Ghost, the most exalted order of chivalry in France. It may seem odd to us but it was his way of honouring the King of Kings; it was an expression of his spirituality.[3]

The purpose of this book is to enrich individual spiritualities of today by bringing them into contact with different aspects of the Christian tradition. Some aspects will suit one person and not another. Here one must follow one's spiritual instinct, in overall obedience to the Gospel, remembering the maxim quoted by Abbot Chapman: 'Pray as you can, and do not try to pray as you can't'.[4]

Secondly, since spirituality is a growing process, it needs guidance, especially in the early stages. That is why, since the time of John Cassian, it has been recognised that a spiritual director is of great importance to someone who wants to advance in the spiritual life.[5] Every candidate to the priesthood and to the religious life has from the beginning of his or her training a spiritual director to whom the heart can be opened in complete confidence. The peer group is inadequate here; it is the guidance of the 'elder' which is needed, one who is both experienced in the tradition of the spiritual writers and in the foibles of the human condition. Similarly, anyone who wants to progress in the spiritual life should start by finding a wise director, priest, religious sister or lay person. Spiritual direction is a particular charism which is much needed in the Church today.

It cannot be emphasised too much that the great danger of the spiritual life is Pharisaism, the conviction that one is better than other people because of one's achievements. This can nullify all spirituality by putting human achievement in the place of divine grace. A false spirituality soon becomes a cover for self-deception and worse. Fr Ken Collins' study of 'the prayer of Jesus' in this book is an essential corrective with its reminder that the recognition of our own poverty is indispensable for man to come before God.

Since the prime mover in the spiritual life is God, it follows that the simplest spirituality can lead to the greatest holiness. Parents who are busy bringing up their children may not have the opportunity to go on retreats but they advance in the spiritual life by doing God's will from day to day and from hour to hour; in the case of parents with small children, that means being at their beck and call most of their waking hours. When St John Marie Vianney came as parish priest to Ars he noticed a peasant who would regularly put down his tools at the door of the church and go in. When the curé asked him what he was doing, he replied: 'I am aware of God and he is aware of me'.[6] That man had had little formal education and he may well have been illiterate but he had obviously reached an advanced state of contemplative prayer.

That being said however, it is true that our society is a complex and sophisticated one. Once the children are in bed, or grown up, the modern parent is subject to the influences of a varied culture. Unlike the parishioner of the Curé of Ars, he has benefited from a secondary as well as a primary education; his children probably know how to operate a computer. Modern man has an enhanced appreciation of the wonderful variety and richness of the created universe, but it is the inner landscape which remains uncharted for him. He is in danger of spiritual famine in the midst of his plenty. That is why these studies have been published. They seek to complement the input of the media

11

and the glossies which seem strangely uninformative where the spiritual life is concerned.

Finally, it is important to remember that there is a sacrament which has a special bearing on the spiritual life; it is called Confirmation. In the revised rite of Confirmation when the bishop stretches out his hands over the candidates, he says a prayer which begins: 'All-powerful God, Father of our Lord Jesus Christ, by water and the Holy Spirit you freed your sons and daughters from sin and gave them new life. Send your Holy Spirit upon them to be their helper and guide'. This expresses both the importance of Baptism and the role of the Holy Spirit in guiding the baptised person. Through Confirmation, the gifts of the Spirit are available for that growth in prayer and action which is the vocation of every Christian. But now there is an inner guide for the journey and another hand on the tiller. The Holy Spirit is not outside us in our spiritual quest; he guides it from within to that friendship with the three persons of the Trinity which is our sharing in the inner life of God.

1

The spirituality of the Old Testament

by
David McGough

> Your word is a lamp for my steps
> and a light for my path[1]
>
> *Psalm 118:105*

The words of Psalm 118 provide a framework for all who seek God through the Scriptures. The spirit of this meditation on God's saving Word is more than an invitation to learning: it is a call to communion with God through and in the Scriptures. The scope of this present chapter is expressed in the continuing words of this same psalm.

> By your word give me life.
> Teach me discernment and knowledge.
> I yearn for your saving help,
> I hope in your word.
>
> *Psalm 118:37,66,81*

The meaning of any word, and especially the Word of God in scripture, demands patient listening. This listening is by no means the preserve of those who are schooled in biblical scholarship. It embraces all those who, in the footsteps of Isaiah's servant, seek to respond to God's call with their lives. Listening is an essential part of discipleship.

> Morning by morning he wakens my ear,
> to hear as those who are taught.
> The Lord has opened my ear,
> and I was not rebellious,
> I turned not backward.
>
> *Isaiah 50:4-5*

---

1. All scripture quotations, with the exception of the Psalms, are from the *RSV*. Quotation of the Psalms are from *The Psalms: A New Translation*, Collins.

The words of the servant guide our reading of the Old Testament. We turn to the Scriptures not to master them, but to be mastered by the God who speaks through their words. To seek for a spirituality of the Old Testament is to reach beyond the limited perception of the mind and be embraced by the knowledge of the heart.

For the Christian the Old Testament does not stand by itself. It is the promise whose fulfilment is Christ Jesus. This does not free us to turn immediately to the pages of the New Testament. To understand Jesus of Nazareth we must understand the Scriptures that expressed the hopes and longings of his world. The faith of the New Testament is the child of the old, and we can never forget that our own lives are the same pilgrimage from promise to fulfilment that is described in the Old Testament and realised in the New.

The Old Testament cannot be read as a single, homogeneous work. It chronicles, over many generations, a faith whose beginning was appropriate to the relatively simple demands of a nomadic people. The survival of this faith was challenged by the changing circumstances of Israel's long history.

The faith of a child is not adequate to the complex demands of the adult. The same is true of the evolving response of the Old Testament scriptures. Israel's response grew as a tribal people reached towards independence as a nation. The blessings and curses of a more sophisticated way of life called for a different understanding of God. The broadening world-view that emerged as Israel became a nation among the nations demanded a correspondingly broader view of Yahweh's claim to be God. Such a development ultimately proclaimed the God of Israel to be the God of all creation. The reverses of her history, no less than the triumphs, colour the expression of this faith. The Old Testament speaks from the rich tapestry of Israel's experience. In consequence it presents not one, but many spiritualities.

Far from creating confusion in those who seek God through Israel's journey, this evolving picture mirrors the experience of every believer. From birth to death life is confronted with an ever-changing situation. The elements of joy and tragedy live together in an uneasy tension. A purely static spirituality cannot reconcile life's conflicting experiences, nor lay foundations for the future. We are called to enter each succeeding experience, and, from such experience, uncover God's purpose in our lives. In this our search is reflected in the Old Testament whose spiritual traditions correspond to the unfolding patterns of Israel's history.

Despite the varied traditions of the Old Testament, there are several constants that speak through its pages. An appreciation of these is not only a guide to our reading; it is also an enrichment of our self-understanding in relationship to God.

One of the more important elements of the semitic mentality is found in the contrast between our modern evaluation of the individual and that which runs throughout the Old Testament. For us the worth of the individual rests in the uniqueness of each personality. Self-esteem flows from the achievements that establish the independence of the individual. This pattern might well serve the aspirations of modern society, but it is a poor guide to humanity's self-understanding before God. The patterns of the Old Testament are quite different. Here the dignity of the individual is located in his belonging to a people summoned by God, rather than in the unique gifts of personality and achievement. The inheritance of Israel is a sense of belonging in which God's blessings to the individual are mediated through the community. The dangerous isolation which can seem to put God beyond the grasp of the individual was broken down in the mutual ties which bound this people to each other in their common vocation. The experience of the People of God in the Old Testament summons us to that sense of belonging which should be the characteristic of every family, parish and church.

A further witness from the Old Testament to contemporary spirituality is to be found in God's constant involvement with his people. The ultimate expression of that involvement is to be found in the incarnation of Jesus Christ. The Old Testament prepared the way for this coming and, in so doing, can heighten our awareness of the dimensions that Christ's coming must assume in our own lives.

The Hebrew Scriptures constantly situate God's presence in the needs and longings of every generation. Their path to God does not lie in an escape from the daily round of life, but in the raising up of that life to God. Consequently the basic models of an Old Testament spirituality are expressed in the historical experience of its people. In the pages that follow we must be content to touch upon three of the most fundamental experiences that formed Israel's religious consciousness. Our concern is not for the detail of history, but for the spirituality that rises from the lived experience of a people. In this the patriarchal history, the Exodus and the establishment of the monarchy will be our guides.

1. The spirituality of the patriarchal history

An initial reading of Genesis, chapters 12-50, might indicate little beyond the fragmented history of a people seeking a foothold on the land. A great deal of what is related seems inconsequential and even disedifying. We are ill at ease with the passages that describe Abraham's ready compromise with the honour of his wife (*Genesis 12:10ff*), and the unseemly quarrels that are generated by his further marriage to Hagar (*Genesis 16:1ff*). Our sense of justice is offended by the triumph of Jacob's deceit over his brother Esau and his kinsman Laban (*Genesis 25:27-34 & chapters 27-31*). The narratives which describe the first footholds in the land through the possession of a well or a burial plot (e.g. *Genesis 26:17-22*) seem to be little more than the footnotes of a remote tribal history. And yet these narratives sanctify the mundane events of life, making them the meeting place of God and man.

The central figures, Abraham, Isaac and Jacob, are not presented for themselves alone. They represent the faithful Israelite of every generation. Their wandering search for a permanent dwelling in the land of Canaan strikes a fundamental chord in the human heart: the need for security and a sense of belonging. The same longing is expressed in the repeated emphasis on the begetting of children whose increase will provide a stable society so necessary for man's security (e.g. *Genesis 15:1-6*).

The patriarchal history is an eloquent witness to the God who reveals himself as Father. Here is a God who is known not only in the sphere of the sacred, but also in the profane. By revealing God in answer to Israel's primitive longing for security of land and offspring, the Old Testament invites a faith that seeks God in the midst of life rather than within the limited confines of what we describe as the sacred. Far from being scandalised by the weakness in Abraham which compromises the honour of Sarah (*Genesis 12:10ff*) in the pursuit of survival, we should be strengthened by the unspoken word that God's purpose is greater than the flawed response of human nature. The images of our own broken response to God's call abound throughout these narratives. In the face of the invitation to become God's people the family of Abraham is divided by petty jealousies; Jacob's deception supplants Esau, and the pride of Joseph calls forth the hatred of his brothers.

These are the pages of our own humanity, and the assurance that God's loving kindness raises up the least attractive aspects of that fallen humanity.

It is apparent from this limited survey of the patriarchal narratives that we are presented with something reaching beyond a history of nomadic origins. We begin to understand why the God of the Fathers was presented in such apparently primitive terms. He was the giver of the land, the protector in war and the guarantor of numerous offspring precisely because his salvation takes man's most basic longings and raises them to something higher.

Many generations made this truth their own in the constant retelling of the stories of Abraham, Isaac and Jacob. Nor was this a simple retelling, for later generations discovered new truths in the history of their origins.

An era of great change in Israel's history contributed its own particular witness in the handing on of the patriarchal traditions. The establishment of the Kingdom under David marked an abrupt transition in the life of a hitherto tribal society. The rights and the privileges of the individual no longer rested in the extended family of the tribal unit. Now the power of a centralised monarchy conflicted with the aspirations of the individual. The God who had seemed adequate to the limited demands of a nomadic existence seemed unequal to the challenges of a world whose horizon had been extended by the achievements of David and Solomon.

We can speculate that the individual's sense of belonging was seriously compromised in a rapidly changing situation. In terms of a nomadic culture, the advent of the monarchy represented the bewildering progress that confronts modern man, and seems to render redundant his previous expressions of God. Such questioning did not abandon the God of the Fathers, but led to an ever deepening insight into the God who was with his people at the dawn of a new and unfamiliar age.

A generation immersed in rapid change stressed the faith of their father Abraham. Abraham had been called to abandon the familiar securities of country, kindred and his father's house (*Genesis 12:1*). The sole ground for his hazardous journey rested in the unknown land that the Lord would reveal to him. It is evident that the unconditional faith demanded of Abraham speaks to the insecurity of a later generation. Such faith was its guide from the trusted ways of the past into the unfamiliar paths of the future. So long as faith reaches from the secure paths of our own choosing to the unknown ways of God's future, the faith of Abraham will always find an echo.

The journey in faith from the old to the new, from self-assurance to an ever opening trust in God, is not without its struggles. Jacob represents that struggle at the heart of faith. The figure of Jacob has its beginnings in the selfish desire to seize and control the material supports of security. The narrative of his deceit (*Genesis 27-32*) reveals the grasping that sets brother against brother and kinsman against kinsman. In Jacob we recognise man struggling for what he can achieve of himself. Such conflict feeds an increasing alienation both from society and from God. The Jacob narrative represents this truth in the episode of Jacob's struggle with the unknown God at Peniel (*Genesis 32: 22ff*).

Later generations, in recounting the story, perceived that salvation does not lie in the pride that seeks to manipulate events for its own gain. It is only when man surrenders the struggle to assert himself that he is open to receive God's salvation as gift. Such is the burden of Jacob's moving entreaty as he lets go a lifetime of deceit.

> O God of my father Abraham and God of my father Isaac, O Lord who didst say to me: 'Return to your country and your kindred and I will do you good'. I am not worthy of the least of all the steadfast love and all the faithfulness which thou hast shown to thy servant, for with only my staff I crossed this Jordan, and now I have become two companies. Deliver me I pray thee. . .
>
> *Genesis 32:9-11*

Only when he is reconciled both to God and his brethren does Jacob enter the promised inheritance. Whether it be Jacob on the banks of the Jordan, Israel confronted with the complexities of her newly founded kingdom, or today's believer seeking direction, the witness of Jacob's prayer remains the same. God's moment of grace lies in the abandonment of inner discord and the acceptance of his deliverance.

The narratives of Abraham, Isaac and Jacob give direction to life in the thread of promise and fulfilment that links them together (e.g. *Genesis 12:1-3; 13:14-16; 17:5ff*). The skilful tapestry which interweaves the nomadic struggle for the land with God's faithful promise silently asserts the ground of salvation. As the Fathers did not win the land, but received it in promise, so salvation is received as gift, but never captured as of right.

> And Abraham believed the Lord, and he reckoned it to him as righteousness.
>
> *Genesis 15:6*

The unfolding of Abraham's faith should not deceive the believer into the impression that trust in God's promised salvation opens an untroubled path to the future. The supreme achievement of Abraham's faith, his rejoicing in Isaac as the continuation of God's faithful promise, leads in a quite unexpected direction. Abraham is called to sacrifice the Son who was the very embodiment of faith and hope.

The narrative of the sacrifice of Isaac (*Genesis 22*) is strange ground for today's reader. The God who demands human sacrifice, even if we are forewarned that this demand is but a test not to be realised, seems far removed from the God of the New Testament. This picture is softened somewhat by the oft repeated observation that the early telling of this story related Yahweh's rejection of child sacrifice as practised in the land of Canaan.

Later generations, however, received and passed on the story with a more profound understanding. There is in man an overwhelming drive to reduce the possibilities of God's promise to that which can be mastered and firmly held. By reducing God's salvation to the narrow compass of his own secure horizons, man reduces the promise to an idol of his own making. This surely gives meaning to the demand that Abraham should sacrifice his son. All his hopes had been focused on this child who would inherit the promise. Isaac's birth seemed to exhaust the generosity of God's self-giving. But Isaac was the gift and not the giver. If Abraham's pilgrimage of faith was to end in the giver himself, he could not be content simply with the gift. In this we glimpse something of the God-forsakenness that enters faith's journey. The symbol of Isaac surrendered in sacrifice speaks to every believer, called to reach beyond the signs of God's presence so as to be captured by the Presence itself. The 'Isaac' in our lives can assume many laudable forms. It may well be a particular person, or a routine of life, a familiar form of prayer or a spirituality that seems to answer our needs. It is through our willingness to forego such signs that God's grace works in us the freedom to receive more abundantly the promise that is ours. The abandonment which is shown in Abraham's surrender interprets every attachment, however worthy, that stands between us and God. The pain of Abraham's abandonment was answered in the joy of the renewed promise:

> By myself I have sworn, says the Lord, because you have done this, and have not withheld your son, your only son, I will indeed bless you and I will multiply your descendants as the stars of heaven and as the sand which is on the seashore.
>
> *Genesis 22:15ff*

The paradox of Abraham's sacrifice reaches forward to the Gospel paradox.

> If any man would come after me, let him deny himself and take up his cross and follow me. For whoever would save his life will lose it, and whoever loses his life for my sake will gain it.
>
> *Matthew 16:24-26*

This single example of the sacrifice of Isaac could well serve as a commentary on the unfolding history of God's people. The supreme sacrifice of Abraham's surrender warned subsequent generations against a static confession which clung to the past at the expense of a future filled with God's promise. The most central assertions of the Old Testament faith were constantly renewed in a surrender that must have been experienced as something close to the sacrifice of all hope. The following example from the developing Exodus tradition will serve to illustrate our own faith.

2. The spirituality of the Exodus deliverance

The essential nature of the Old Testament faith is revealed in the Exodus event. The transcendent God is revealed as the truly personal God who encounters his people on the level of their need.

> I have seen the affliction of my people who are in Egypt, and have heard their cry because of their taskmasters; I know their sufferings, and I have come to deliver them out of the hand of the Egyptians, and to bring them up out of that land to a good and broad land, a land flowing with milk and honey.
>
> *Exodus 3:7-8*

Only the most superficial reading of Exodus can satisfy itself with the conclusion that it relates the remote origins of national deliverance, and is therefore of no more than historical interest to today's reader.

The Old Testament reaches beyond the historical particularity of the Exodus to express the faith of succeeding generations, for whom God's deliverance was an ever present reality. The annual celebration of the Exodus in the Jewish Passover was rooted in the bondage of Egypt. Its promise of deliverance, however, was addressed to the succeeding bonds of a people enslaved by their own infidelity and injustice. For this reason the instructions that direct the Passover celebration are not a nostalgic reminiscence of the past: they are the joyful assertion of a God whose vitality brings deliverance to the present moment. Hence such instructions make no distinction between past and present, between the bondage of Egypt and the succeeding enslavements which hinder man's journey towards God. All generations are as one before the God whose deliverance hears and responds to their cry for freedom.

> Remember this day, in which you came out of Egypt,
> out of the house of bondage, for by strength of hand
> the Lord brought you out from this place. . .
>
> *Exodus 13:3*

Insofar as we, the new children of Israel, stand in need of deliverance, we can sing the psalms of Israel's deliverance (e.g. Psalms 114 and 115) in celebration of the freedom that is ours in Christ Jesus:

> Some lay in darkness and in gloom,
> prisoners in misery and chains. . .
> Then they cried to the Lord in their need
> and he rescued them from their distress.
> He led them forth from darkness and gloom
> and broke their chains to pieces.
> Let them thank the Lord for his goodness,
> for the wonders he does for men.
>
> *Psalm 107:10,13-15*

In both narrative and psalm, the Old Testament invites us to live in the real presence of God's saving events. Just as the Exodus was an active presence rather than a past event, so the death and resurrection of Christ is a living presence rather than a past event.

We learn much from the constant retelling of the Exodus event and the subsequent enrichment of its meaning. Scholarship indicates that the songs of Moses and Miriam contain elements of the earliest celebration of Israel's deliverance. Their expression conveys all the joy of new-found freedom. We should not be offended by the language that speaks of God as a mighty warrior, for such was Israel's greatest need in the precarious journey from enslavement to nationhood.

> I will sing to the Lord, for he has triumphed gloriously,
> the horse and the rider he has thrown into the sea
>
> *Exodus 15:1,21*

The triumphalism of this early faith carried with it dangers that were demonstrated all too clearly in Israel's later history. The proclamation of deliverance became ossified into a confidence that was indifferent to the demands of God's justice in daily life. The Exodus came to be seen as the guarantee of future salvation. The demands of the Covenant, summoning man to the service of God and neighbour, were forgotten in this proud boast. Israel's salvation lay not in the boast of the Exodus, but in the response that it both summoned and enabled. In like manner the enduring value of any spirituality is expressed in its lived response to God's grace.

21

Throughout her history Israel was confronted with the disparity between the gracious God of the Exodus and the infidelity of her own response. The judgement voiced by the prophets caused her to ponder anew the central mystery of the Exodus. The book of Deuteronomy relates the Exodus event from the insight of mature reflection and the passage of many generations. The proud boast of Moses' song of victory has been tempered by the prophetic judgement on a faithless people. The pattern of Israel's past deliverance provides the model for the conversion to which she is summoned. Consequently the narrative framework of Deuteronomy sets Moses' proclamation of the law on the very threshold of the Promised Land. The past which Moses recalls interprets the present moment of God's grace to his people.

> For you are a people holy to the Lord your God; the Lord your God has chosen you to be a people for his own possession out of all the peoples who are on the face of the earth. It was not because you were more in number than any other people that the Lord set his love upon you and chose you, for you were the least of all peoples; but it was because the Lord loves you, and is keeping the oath which he swore to your fathers, that the Lord has brought you out with mighty hand, and redeemed you from the house of bondage, from the hand of Pharaoh, king of Egypt.
>
> *Deuteronomy 7:6-8*

The future, no less than the past, is made to proclaim the abundance of God's grace. The inheritance of this people will be found in cities 'which you did not build'; in cisterns 'which you did not hew'; in vineyards and olives 'which you did not plant'. (*cf. Deuteronomy 6:10-12*)

The thrust of Deuteronomy is expressed in the 'today' so often on the lips of Moses. This day represents the 'today' of every generation as it acknowledges God's loving kindness and is summoned to take possession of its promised inheritance. Long reflection interpreted life's every moment as the graced response which stands between God's deliverance and its full realisation. The infidelity of Israel's past did not detract from that moment. Such infidelity highlighted the choice that confronted each moment of Israel's faith.

> See, I have set before you this day life and good, death and evil. If you obey the commandments of the Lord your God, by walking in his ways, by keeping his commandments and his statutes and his ordinances,

> then you shall live and multiply, and the Lord your
> God will bless you in the land where you are entering
> to take possession of it.
>
> *Deuteronomy 30:15-16*

Thus the book of Deuteronomy presents the ancient Exodus tradition in a new light. The focus has moved from the yesterday of Israel's history to the today of the hearer's response. The pilgrim church is no less summoned by Christ's death and resurrection. In Christ our deliverance is achieved. The 'today' of our response opens to the promised inheritance of his kingdom.

3. The spirituality of the kingdom, Jerusalem and the messianic promises

Two concluding examples of Old Testament spirituality, both embodying the changing course of history, underline the flexibility of Israel's faith. We are reminded that the diversity of Israel's experience is matched by the creative diversity of her spirituality. Today's disciple is cautioned against the narrowed vision which seeks to restrict the abundance of God's grace to the expression of any one spirituality.

The celebration of the Exodus, which we have considered above, had its beginnings in the social conditions of a tribal and nomadic people. As such, the deliverance and subsequent occupation of the land presented God to Israel in a language that spoke directly to her aspirations.

The conquest and settlement, however, promoted expectations different from those of a nomadic people. The book of Judges draws our attention to the causes of these different expectations through its description of Israel's fragile hold upon the land in the early years of settlement. The loosely knit confederation of tribes, despite its occasional victories, was no match for the well-disciplined forces of the Philistine city states that had threatened Israel's existence from its very beginning.

The monarchy, such a radical departure from tribal ways, was the key to survival. Nothing less than the coordination of tribal interests under a central ruler could ensure the survival of the people. The capital city would be the focus for the emerging sense of national unity that would arm the tribes of Israel against their common enemy. The painful transition to dynastic rule, and its first stumbling steps with Saul, are described in the first book of Samuel. Only under the charismatic leadership of David, continued in the expansion of Solomon's kingdom, did Israel emerge with the full confidence of an independent kingdom.

The historical details of this emergence need not delay us here. What is of concern is the interaction of these events with Israel's conception of her relationship with God.

The throne secured by David, together with the newly conquered Jerusalem which served as the centre of his administration, became something more than the achievements of an emerging kingdom. For past generations the Exodus, or the call of Israel's tribal ancestors, had provided the models for God's continuing presence. Now, in a different era, the Davidic King and his royal city proclaimed the same saving presence. The God who walked with Abraham, Isaac and Jacob, who had delivered his people through the hand of Moses, now established the Davidic line as the sign and instrument of his presence. The book of Samuel describes the covenant which established David's rule as the sacrament of God's blessing on his people (cf. *2 Samuel 7*). The prayer of the Psalms witnesses to the veneration of God's kingdom and rule in the person of David and his successors.

> I have found David my servant
> and with my holy oil anointed him.
> My hand shall always be with him
> and my arm shall make him strong.
> I will keep my love for him always.
> He will say to me: 'You are my Father,
> my God, the rock who saves me'.
> And I will make him my first born,
> the highest of the kings of the earth.
>
> *Psalm 89: 20-21,26-27*

This exalted celebration of the King was equally a celebration of all God's people, for they, no less than the king as their embodiment, were the first born who turned to God as father.

What was said of the Davidic kingship was also said of Jerusalem. She also became the symbol and means of God's presence among his people.

> For the Lord has chosen Zion;
> He has desired it for his dwelling:
> This is my resting place for ever,
> Here I have chosen to live.
>
> I will greatly bless her produce,
> I will fill her poor with bread,
> I will clothe her priests with salvation
> and her faithful shall ring out their joy.
>
> *Psalm 132:13-16*

Western thought-patterns, which are more at home with abstract expressions of our relationship with God, do not readily accept language which situates this relationship in the royal line and Jerusalem as its capital.

Further reflection is encouraged by the observation that the God of the Old Testament is no abstraction. He enters the very life of his people, raising the Davidic kingship from its beginnings in national expediency to become the expression of his presence. In this lies the promise that God identifies himself with the needs of his people. Yahweh, who spoke through Israel's need for a king, speaks through the continuing need of those who turn to him.

The covenant with David, like the covenant with Moses, summoned the response of the people. Consequently Jerusalem and its divinely appointed king, the symbols of God's ruling presence, became the figures of Israel's infidelity. Kings who had been called to establish God's justice among the nations fell short of their calling. The pride of power and affluence obscured their dependence on the God whose covenant had established Israel's throne. Acquisitive greed trampled the rights of the poor and needy whose protection was the particular concern of Israel's anointed kings. The desire to placate and imitate the rulers of other nations seriously compromised the integrity of the nation's faith. It was the particular tragedy of Israel's kings to be torn between two conflicting ideals. Was their security to be found in the promises that had established David's line, or in the achievements of human power and political intrigue?

From the eighth century BC onwards the prophets of Israel (Amos, Hosea, Isaiah, Jeremiah) voiced God's judgment on the faithlessness of the royal houses. Jerusalem, once the symbol of God's righteousness, became the symbol of infidelity.

> How the faithful city
> has become a harlot,
> she that was full of justice!
> Righteousness lodged in her,
> but now murderers.
> Your silver has become dross,
> your wine mixed with water.
> Your princes are rebels
> and companions of thieves.
> Every one loves a bribe
> and runs after gifts.
> They do not defend the fatherless,
> and the widow's cause does not come to them.
>
> *Isaiah 1:21-23*

Subsequent generations were challenged by the prophetic word to recognise in themselves the tragic compromise denounced in Zion's rebel princes. Human expediency is ever tempted to compromise the absolute demands of divine sovereignty, and in the broken trust of Israel's kings we see the reflection of our own sinfulness.

Such compromise seemed to lead to the death of all hope when the power of Babylon ended the Davidic line, destroying Jerusalem and leading its inhabitants into exile. These catastrophic events of the sixth century BC were more than a dramatic change in the national fortunes. They questioned the existence of the God who had been revealed in the deliverance of the Exodus, who had established his people in the land and raised up kings as the sign of his enduring favour. The course of events seemed to indicate that either this God was powerless to save, or that he had totally rejected his people. The prayer of Lamentations captures something of the inner desolation that accompanied the fall of Jerusalem.

> I am the man who has seen affliction
> under the rod of his wrath;
> he has driven me and brought me
> into the wilderness without any light;
> surely against me he turns his hand
> again and again the whole day long.
>
> *Lamentations 3:1-3*

These verses describe the spiritual wilderness that overwhelmed Israel following the destruction of Jerusalem. It was a wilderness that proved to be among the most creative experiences in her relationship with God. The history of the monarchy had demonstrated the fragility of human commitment. Israel was confronted with her own poverty, and from the poverty of her response she was led from the proud independence of the monarchy to rest in God alone.

> Put no trust in princes,
> in mortal men in whom there is no help.
> Take their breath, they return to clay,
> and their plans that day come to nothing.
>
> He is happy who is helped by Jacob's God,
> whose hope is in the Lord alone.
>
> *Psalm 146:3-5*

The promises that lay in the ruins of Jerusalem were raised to life in messianic expectation. Far from coming to an end, the promises to David would find their fulfilment in one whom the Lord himself would raise up. What had seemed like rejection was a new beginning. The destitution of kingly rulers called forth a rule that would rest in the power of God's own spirit.

> There shall come forth a shoot
> from the stump of Jesse,
> and a branch shall grow out of his roots.
> And the spirit of the Lord shall rest upon him,
> and the spirit of wisdom and understanding,
> the spirit of counsel and might,
> the spirit of knowledge and fear of the Lord.
> And his delight shall be in the fear of the Lord.
>
> *Isaiah 11:1-3*

These prophetic words, spoken against the imminent bankruptcy of a faithless kingdom, transform the hopes of every broken generation. The crisis of the exile did not lead to the abandonment of the promise, but to its broader interpretation. The one who was to rule Israel would enter the heart of her suffering, and in his own person witness to God's healing presence.

> He was wounded for our transgressions,
> he was bruised for our iniquities;
> upon him was the chastisement that
> made us whole, and with his stripes
> we are healed.
>
> *Isaiah 53:5*

For the Christian these words find their fullness in Christ's redemptive suffering. We should never forget that before Christ's coming they spoke from the experience of Israel's desolation, and transformed that desolation into new hope. The trust in earthly princes was increasingly focused on the Messianic figure who would embody the ideals abandoned by the Davidic line.

> The Spirit of the Lord God is upon me,
> Because the Lord has anointed me
> to bring good news to the afflicted;
> He has sent me to bind up the broken hearted,
> to proclaim liberty to the captives,
> and the opening of the prison to those who are bound;
> to proclaim the year of the Lord's favour.
>
> *Isaiah 61:1-2*

The desolation of acknowledged sin was the catalyst that transformed Israel's limited expectations of an earthly ruler into the boundless expectation of a messianic king. In like manner the significance of Jerusalem was ultimately enriched through the tragedy of her destruction. The arrogance of the old Jerusalem was humbled, thereby giving place to the new Jerusalem which proclaimed God's salvation to all mankind.

> Come, let us go up to the mountain of the Lord,
> to the house of the God of Jacob;
> that he may teach us his ways
> and that we might walk in his paths.
> For out of Zion shall go forth the law,
> and the word of the Lord from Jerusalem.
> He shall judge between nations, and shall decide
>   for many peoples;
> and they shall beat their swords into ploughshares,
> and their spears into pruning hooks;
> nation shall not lift up sword against nation,
> neither shall they learn war any more.
>
> *Isaiah 2:3-4*

The hopes expressed in these passages reach into the New Testament, whose risen Lord is acknowledged as the Son of David (e.g. Romans 1:1-6). The triumph of his kingdom is described as the new Jerusalem come down to earth (Revelation 10:10ff).

The messianic development of the Zion and David traditions illustrates the dialogue between Israel's history and her spirituality. Our conclusion must point to a spirituality sharply attuned to the developing needs of the present generation. There can be no other path for a faith that is centred in the Incarnate Word.

Such a direction does not point us to untested innovation for its own sake. The spirituality of the Old Testament constantly reinterpreted ancient traditions in the light of a new experience. In like manner the following chapters of this work sustain contemporary Christianity from its traditional roots.

It has not been the intention of this chapter to present a comprehensive treatment of Old Testament spirituality. Much of importance must remain unsaid. The more modest claims of this chapter are realised if the reader is brought to share the joy so clearly expressed in the Letter to the Hebrews.

> In many and various ways God spoke of old to our
> fathers by the prophets; but in these last days he has
> spoken to us by a Son, whom he appointed the heir
> of all things, through whom he also created the world.
>
> *Hebrews 1:1-2*

2

The prayer of Jesus

by
Kenneth Collins

I think the way to look at the prayer of Jesus is the same as the way we should look at his ethical teaching; it is not a question of looking for rules. What we find is an invitation to look at the world through his eyes, to make his world-vision our own and to live accordingly. If we approach the prayer of Jesus in this way (and in this study I intend to leave out the *Our Father*) we must look first at his vision of God and of man-before-God. We can only understand his prayer once we have made his outlook our own and live before God accordingly.

Jesus' vision of God

One of the most surprising aspects of Jesus' ministry is how little he spoke or taught about himself. He does not thrust himself forward and say 'I am divine; believe in me'. At the heart of his message was the Kingdom of God, not an area or a territory but an activity of God. The Kingdom is there in the context of miraculous activity; when the blind see, the lame dance, the leper is cleansed, God is actively ruling. God calls to wholeness and integrity and begins to reign in lives which were fragmented by sickness and sin. In the ministry of Jesus the light shines, the harvest is ready, the new wine is offered, God's peace is extended to men. It is the dawn of a new age; God has begun to reign 'even now'.[1]

This active rule of God is not confined to the miraculous activity of Jesus in Palestine. It is found also in his teaching which is deliberately designed to jolt the hearer out of his everyday world and to thrust him into living with a new logic under boundless skies. Thus the parable of the Labourers in the Vineyard does not only sound the death-knell of the religion of achievement; it also commands men to live out their lives before a God who is blind to merit. From now on, no one need earn our friendship, forgiveness or concern. We are invited to make this reality of God our own; that is his active claim as king in our lives.

When we examine even more closely the implications of the way in which Jesus sees God's rule breaking out, it becomes clear that we stand before a God of unconditional demand. His claim on man is absolute, though expressed in a variety of ways. Thus the rich young man who wishes to share in eternal life is told: 'You lack one thing; go, sell what you have, and give to the poor, and you will have treasure in heaven; and come follow me' (*Mark 10:21*). 'Treasure in heaven' is a way of saying 'being rich in God's eyes'. Jesus is saying that to be rich in God's eyes demands a radical break with all ties of past and present which contribute to human security. It is all or nothing, a vocation to radical insecurity: 'Thou and thou only. . .'.

Hyperbole and paradox play an important part in Jesus' description of man's reaction when faced with the unconditional demand of God's active rule. The New Age demands that each person go beyond himself and live in a world whose horizons are unlimited and whose territory is invaded by unreasoning and unbounded love. 'If any one would sue you and take your coat, let him have your cloak as well' (*Matthew 5:40*). That it was illegal to retain a poor man's cloak after nightfall and that therefore someone confronted by the kingdom should not stand on even his recognised rights is important enough, but almost peripheral for understanding this saying. Its implementation to the letter would result in imprisonment for indecent exposure, the coat and the cloak being the only two garments worn by men in the Palestine of the day.[2] In other words, when men are faced with God as King, that marks the end of prudential morality, closed options, fixed ideas; it is a new world in which we are swept from our feet, driven only by the absolute claim of the God who calls us.

It is precisely the enervating effect of rules upon this, the all-too human desire to live well-signposted lives securely, which evokes again and again Jesus' impatience with law. 'You leave the commandment of God, and hold fast the tradition of men' (*Mark 7:8*). We can fulfil that demand, satisfy that requirement. There is the tragedy; law has made God safe. We can cope at last; the process of domestication has begun. But the way man should react when overtaken by the dawn of this New Age and shaken out of his attempt to make a comfortable wholeness of his living is to be found in Jesus' vision of man-before-God; it is the prayer reaction.

Jesus' vision of man-before-God

The basic condition which is indispensable for man to come before God in any way is the recognition of his own poverty. This requirement is thematic throughout the ministry of Jesus; he announced the good news to the poor but only to the poor. It may be illustrated clearly by those well-known and loved parables which typify his approach. The account of the Labourers in the Vineyard hinges on the fact that justice and mercy are incompatible. Labour relations which rely upon reward for achievement are destroyed irreparably when unmerited generosity is allowed a place. Payment is made without regard to productivity; God is blind to merit. It is only if there is the recognition that we bring nothing with us when we come near to God and that we are empty-handed in his eyes that an approach is possible at all.

That this is no exaggeration can be demonstrated from the Pharisee and the Publican at prayer in the Temple (*Luke 18:9-14*).[3] The Lucan setting is manifestly artificial and the story has nothing to do with pride versus humility, as we are accustomed to think. Two life-styles are placed side by side, one which is accepted as good and one which is manifestly evil. The good not only fulfils the legal requirements but moves into the area of supererogation. Fasting was demanded once a year but the Pharisee did so twice a week, for the removal of sins and the redemption of Israel; in other words he is concerned about the welfare of others, interceding for sinners before God. Tithes were used normally for distribution to the poor and so his extra self-denial is aimed to help the less fortunate in Israel, a form of alms-giving. His prayer, too, has nothing to do with self-congratulation as can be seen from comparison with other pharisaic prayers available to us from the time; it is a form of first century *Te Deum* for mercies received.

Against this picture of human holiness is placed that of the dissolute, a Jew who had 'made himself a gentile' by working for the Romans, one whose mere glance through a window was enough to contaminate the whole house. Here was a man whose occupation actually hindered God's saving plan for Israel and one for whom repentance in any real meaning of the word would have been impossible; and to remove him even further from redemption, he refuses to pray. That is the meaning of 'would not even lift up his eyes to heaven'. He will not appeal to God. The cry 'God, be merciful to me, a sinner' is the spontaneous articulation of his lostness and despair, rather than a recognised prayer-formula for forgiveness. Yet it is that man who leaves with God's favour and not the other. As J. Jeremias says in the splendid conclusion to his commentary on the parable: the character of God is such that 'he welcomes the despairing hopeless sinner . . . he is the God of the despairing, and for the broken heart his mercy is boundless'.[4] Recognised poverty is the only gateway to God. The Jewish, indeed the ordinary human, reaction to this is illustrated by Jesus himself in recounting the parable of the Prodigal Son (*Luke 15:11-32*). That recognition of lostness should bring the morally and spiritually dead to life and favour in the Father's eyes without any form of satisfaction for past infidelities is too much for the elder son to bear. He cannot rejoice, and this will always be the case when the new vision which we are invited to share remains alien.

To approach God in prayer therefore we must come with empty hands, no deeds well done, no claims which we must satisfy. A section from *The Great Divorce* by C.S. Lewis paints the picture well:[5]

> 'Look at me, now', said the Ghost, slapping its chest. 'I gone straight all my life. I don't say I was a religious man and I don't say I had no faults, far from it. But I done my best all my life, see? I done my best by everyone, that's the sort of chap I was. I never asked for anything that wasn't mine by rights. If I wanted a drink I paid for it and if I took my wages I done my job, see? That's the sort I was and I don't care who knows it. . . . But I got to have my rights same as you, see?'
>
> 'Oh, no, it's not so bad as that. I haven't got my rights, or I should not be here. You will not get yours either. You'll get something far better. Never fear.'
>
> 'That's just what I say. I haven't got my rights, I always done my best and I never done nothing wrong. And what I don't see is why I should be put below a bloody murderer like you.'
>
> 'Who knows whether you will be? Only be happy and come with me.'
>
> 'What do you keep on arguing for? I'm only telling you the sort of chap I am. I only want my rights. I'm not asking for anybody's bleeding charity.'
>
> 'Then do. At once. Ask for the Bleeding Charity. Everything here is for the asking and nothing can be bought.'

When we discover our poverty as the springboard for our prayer, we discover that access to God is *immediate*. In his own prayer and in teaching others to pray, Jesus spoke to God in Aramaic and not in Hebrew, the sacred language. In no way therefore does man have to 'move aside' from the everyday in order to make contact with God. God is to be approached in the language of the home, the market place and the street corner; we are to start from the things that matter to us as human beings, from the ordinary. Thus does Jesus counter the contemporary overemphasis on the transcendence and the distance of God.

But there are further implications; it was a current belief among the Jews that certain externals could separate a man from God; the 'secular' could pull a person away from the 'sacred'. Thus certain foods, particular tools used at work, different forms of sickness, were all obstacles to divine encounter and needed to be ritually purified so that they would no longer distance from God.[6] It is this distinction which Jesus denies absolutely in such sayings as: 'there is nothing outside a man which by going into him can defile him; but the things which come out of a man are what defile him' (*Mark 7:15*). There is no external circumstance, either in the world or in human life, which can separate a man from God; only his own attitude or behaviour can do that. In other words, everything we meet in our daily lives, however neutral or adverse it seems, is meant to be a vehicle to God, provided that we do not abuse it for selfish purposes. This is entirely consistent with the general biblical view that God *extravenes*, i.e. comes out of the human situation which is pregnant with his presence, rather than *intervenes*, by somehow interfering with the course of human history to attract man's attention in some way. Nothing therefore is ever closed to us in our meeting with God; every aspect of life is a door which will open into his presence if we do not ignore it as too ordinary. If we have this vision of reality, the words of the poet Blake take on another meaning:

> To see the world in a grain of sand
> and heaven in a wild flower,
> To hold infinity in the palm of your hand
> and eternity in an hour.

Reality, the family, the home, the place of work, the hand of friendship, the caress of the lover, are all gateways to God; there is no need to 'step aside' in our search for him; even the words we use should come from the heart of our living.

If we accept our own poverty in the approach to God, and also his accessibility through the ordinary, in the words we use at home, it should come as no surprise that our approach should be that of a child. From the evidence we have in the New Testament, we can see that Jesus spoke to God as *Abba*, 'Father', when he prayed and he encouraged his followers to do the same. We shall not grasp the significance of this unless we realise that

Abba was the usual Aramaic word used in the home by a child addressing its father; the little boy or girl would have said *Abba*, 'Father' as it said *Imma*, 'Mother'.

The use of *Abba* for addressing God in prayer seems to have been unique to Jesus, for nowhere else in the Old Testament or in the inter-testamental literature is there a clear example of anyone addressing God as *Abba*. This indicates that Jesus saw himself as standing head and shoulders above his contemporaries in his relationship with God and possessing a unique bond whose only meaningful analogue is that of the parent-child relationship in the human home. Because Jesus encouraged his followers to speak to God in the same way, it follows that he wanted them to relate to him in the same way. We are 'sons in the Son'; his vision and approach to the Father should be ours, with all the implications which flow from this. These implications are clear from his general teaching.

'In praying do not heap up empty phrases as the Gentiles do; for they think they will be heard for their many words' (*Matthew 6:7*). This is frequently taken to mean that the followers of Jesus are released from that 'babbling' of adults who are unsure of themselves when they appear before an employer or king; we should have a still confidence in the access to God which sonship gives us. While this may be true, there is nevertheless another dimension to this saying of Jesus which is of deeper significance and is revealed under further investigation. When many pagans prayed, they considered it necessary to use all the titles of the deities which they approached. To omit the name of a god would not only have rendered the petition useless; it would have incurred the wrath of the god as well. The altar 'to an unknown god' found by Paul at Athens (*Acts 17:32*) is connected with this mentality; to omit a title would be unwise but to forget a god entirely would be disastrous.

Man must always play safe in his relations with the divine. That is the very point which Jesus wishes to make here. In our prayer to the Father there is no need whatsoever to play safe. The ground does not have to be prepared so that we present our most acceptable face, as we would in a job interview during the recession. We can go (back) to God with the same certainty of compassion and understanding as the child throwing itself into its parents' arms. With someone who loves us there is no place for the 'just in case'.

There are many parables which illustrate that when we draw near to God with this child-like confidence, we are certain of gaining a hearing. The Friend at Midnight (*Luke 11:5-8*), the Loving Father (*Luke 11:11-13*), the Unjust Judge and the Widow

(*Luke 18:1-9*) all bear witness to this fact. But what are we to make of the unmistakable promise contained in Our Lord's words: 'Truly I say to you, whoever says to this mountain ''Be taken up and cast into the sea'', and does not doubt in his heart . . . it will be done for him. Therefore I tell you, whatever you ask in prayer, believe that you receive it and you will' (*Mark 11:23-4*).

The moving of mountains is an expression known in certain rabbinic circles and connected with the poem in Isaiah 2:2-4: 'It shall come to pass in the latter days that the mountain of the house of the Lord shall be established as the highest of the mountains and shall be raised above the hills. . .'. The text was seen as a description of the End Time when God's rule will extend throughout the world with Jerusalem as its centre. The Temple, situated on Mount Sion, will be visible to all men everywhere, drawing them to exchange sword for ploughshare and become recipients of the divine peace.

The poetic description was taken literally by many Jews and, because the earth was thought to be flat, they expected a physical growth of the hill on which the temple was built. The three most important mountains in Palestine would be joined together to form an enormous Everest, visible from every part of the world. This picture became a symbol for the dawning of the End Time which would usher in peace, forgiveness, nourishment and healing for all mankind. So the moving of mountains was an expression which conjured up for the Jew the idea of the golden age, the time when God's final gifts would be on offer, when redemption would be available without merit, and forgiveness and sustenance within reach of everyone who stretched out a hand. *That* is what Jesus promises with regard to prayer. Whenever we ask for a gift of the End Time, for something which makes God's redemptive presence real for mankind, then that prayer is infallible. About winning the pools or repaying the mortgage, Jesus promises nothing but he affirms that the healing powers of God's active rule are at work in the world through our prayers.

We draw near in our poverty with empty hands. As children, without having to play safe we approach with confidence to a Father who will infallibly answer the only requests that matter, that we ourselves and others may find healing at his hands. But above all we advance as *human*, with everything which that entails. The circumscription of our lives is not miraculously removed but transcended from within.

All the biblical evidence converges to show that Jesus, when he was faced with the betrayal of his friends, the hostility of the authorities and the certainty of impending death, prayed to God in Gethsemane: '*Abba*, Father . . . remove this cup from me' (*Mark 14:26*). He asked to be spared and yet he was forced to undergo a public and humiliating death. In other words prayer (and here we are dealing with the Perfect Petitioner) does not allow Jesus or us to approach God as some sort of celestial aspirin, something that we can take to make the pain of living go away. He will not provide the escape from human life, with all its weakness, dangers, sufferings, limitations and question marks. God is not a bolt hole down which we can escape the less pleasant consequences of being human. Pain and loss, chance and circumstance, the limited horizons and the claustrophobic boundaries of our lives, they all remain.

Why then should we pray? What difference does our prayer make if God refuses to play the great magician when he is presented with our lostness? It is in Luke's footnote to the prayer in Gethsemane that we find the answer: 'and there appeared to him an angel from heaven strengthening him' (*Luke 22:43*). The divine reply is to help man to go through rather than circumvent what it means to be human. It is by embracing everything which goes to make up the human condition that we emerge renewed.

It is easy to consider this suggestion as evasive, but this is not the case. The way in which the early Christians resolved the problem is evidenced from *Hebrews 5:7*: 'in the days of his flesh Jesus offered up prayers and supplications, with loud cries and tears, to him who was able to save him from death, and *he was heard* for his godly fear'. Far therefore from presenting the Christian with a problem, the prayer in Gethsemane was considered as having been heard and Jesus' request as having been granted. But how? The thought is simple to follow. Jesus asked to be saved from death, but he died. Some time later came the resurrection through which he entered a state where death could never again be on the remotest horizon. From now on it was meaningless; it had been annihilated; it was no longer a constitutive factor of his being human. As such it was a request which, in its fullness, could never have been part of any human conscious request in the real world. And yet a prayer to be saved from death is answered by the gift of eternal freedom from death beyond the wildest dream of the petitioner. By being fully human, Jesus emerged renewed. Humanity undenied has become a vehicle for the kingdom.

Prayerful contact with God, therefore, thrusts us deeper into the reality of being human. Nothing, perhaps, illustrates the weakness and fumbling of man better than his propensity to make mistakes, to get it wrong again and again. Jesus himself spent the whole night in prayer before choosing the Twelve, and then picked Judas.

Whatever prayer may do, therefore, it does not stop us making mistakes from a human point of view; no one would deliberately choose as an intimate companion a person who could clearly be foreseen as a betrayer. Prayer cannot release us from the normal considerations of prudence before decision-making; careless preparation will still be responsible for sloppy results.

Far from making us question the value of prayer before the more significant decisions and events of our lives, such a conclusion should be seen as positive. For anyone who is trying to make his own the outlook or world view of Jesus, what is termed a mistake from a human point of view seems to be a common denominator in God's dealing with us. In all his undertakings with man at the most pivotal times of their personal and national history, God always seems to have a predilection for choosing persons and means which men and women regard as incompatible with the task in hand, the weak, the inappropriate, the human failure. Thus the elderly Abraham and the sterile Sarah are chosen as parents of Israel; the youngest son of the weakest clan (Gideon) is to save God's people from the Midianite invasion which threatens the very existence of the nation; the prejudiced and embittered Pharisee (Paul) is to spread the message of mercy and grace throughout the world; the cross, an instrument which guaranteed hell to all Jewish believers, is to become the symbol of salvation.

The theology of failure, if we may so term it, dominates God's dealing with man. It is against this background, therefore, that the choice of Judas must be seen; through the traitor God could work, even though his original selection by Jesus did not correspond to human norms and was mistaken even in the eyes of the one who selected him ('It would have been better for that man if he had not been born', *Mark 14:21*). From every 'mistake', therefore, which flows from a situation of prayer, God will bring good, the advance of the kingdom. But, unless we share his vision, the prayer will seem unanswered.

Central to Jesus' life and teaching in Palestine was his Father's rule, that activity of God which draws men and women to live with a new vision of the world around them and to grow into the giants they were all intended to be, not by any short cuts or magic but by becoming more human than they have ever dared to be before. That invitation is open to us; the active reign of God can be made present in and through our lives; we can become centres of heaven on earth. There is only one condition, we must begin and continue to pray.

3

The spirituality of the desert fathers

by
Austin Hughes

The desert fathers were people who lived in a time of crisis. The Roman world of the fourth century was threatened by invasion from without and moral and economic collapse from within.

This may sound surprising to those who remember that the fourth century was the time of official conversion of the Roman Empire to Christianity. But the conversion of Constantine in 313 did not bring about a deep-rooted or widespread conversion overnight. Under Constantine, Christian priests were granted the same privileges and financial rewards as the old pagan priests, and these new privileges were a mixed blessing. Within a couple of decades, the popular charges of corruption, embezzlement and self-seeking, so often levelled against pagan priests, began to be made against Christian priests too.

But the crisis was not simply about a few clerics on the make. The Roman Empire's security was threatened by barbarian invasions from the north, famines and a crisis of confidence from within. In Constantine's youth, Imperial Rome's flagging fortunes were blamed on the ineffectiveness of the old Imperial gods. New cults and mystery religions flourished, in the hope that prosperity would be restored. Constantine himself flirted with sun-worship, an eastern religion, before finally settling for another eastern religion: Christianity.

The political and social background, then, of the early fourth century, was one of upheaval; religious upheaval, political instability and financial insecurity. During Constantine's reign, the political capital of the empire was transferred from Rome to Nicomedia in Asia-minor, as the western half of the Empire became more and more unsettled.

The desert fathers first appeared in the Egyptian desert around the year 300 AD. The Egyptian desert was not the only desert to attract monks and hermits. There were others in Palestine and Syria. But the Egyptian desert areas of Scetis and Nitria (Northern Egypt, about forty miles south-west of Alexandria) were the ones that became most famous, and about which most was written. The writers were not desert fathers themselves but usually city ecclesiastics. The desert fathers as a rule left no written works behind, and some even took pride in being illiterate. In their view, writing was the work of idle, academic philosophers!

We know of the desert fathers from what others have written about them — from Athanasius, John Cassian, Evagrius, Palladius, Rufinus, and others who drew on the wisdom of the desert for the edification of people elsewhere. There are also anonymous collections of the sayings of the desert fathers that exist in various versions, and tell of the teaching of individual fathers.

These sayings probably circulated in an oral tradition for several years before ever being edited in a written form. This should lead us to be a little cautious when we are investigating the spirituality of the desert fathers. The theological or moral unity of the various collections of sayings probably comes from the *editors* and not from the fathers themselves. When reading about them we should always recollect that we are seeing them through the lenses of a Cassian or an Athanasius, who were naturally preoccupied with the theological and ecclesiastical struggles of their own locality, and did not hesitate to draw on the reputation of a desert father or two if it would advance their cause.

This chapter will draw mainly on the *Alphabetical Collection of the Sayings of the Desert Fathers* (so called because each father is listed in order according to the Greek alphabet) collected and edited by an unknown author in the fifth century. It is a collection of wise sayings and short stories designed to instruct and edify the reader. A few examples will help to show the tone of the collection.

> Abba John the Dwarf said, 'A house is not built by beginning at the top and working down. You must begin with the foundations in order to reach the top.' They said to him, 'What does this saying mean?' He said, 'The foundation is our neighbour, whom we must win, and that is the place to begin. For all the commandments of Christ depend on this one'.[1]

This is a simple short episode designed to remind people of fundamentals. A story of Poeman the Shepherd illustrated the desert fathers' love of homely images.

39

A brother said to Abba Poemen, 'Give me a word,' and he said to him, 'As long as the pot is on the fire, no fly or any animal can get near it, but as soon as it is cold, these creatures get inside. So it is for the monk; as long as he lives in spiritual activities, the enemy cannot find a means of overthrowing him'.[2]

Sometimes the stories could be directed against specific sins. A story about Moses the Black is directed against racism.

Another day, a council was being held in Scetis, the Fathers treated Moses with contempt in order to test him, saying, 'Why does this black man come among us?' When he heard this he kept silence. When the council was dismissed, they said to him, 'Abba, did that not grieve you at all?' He said to them, 'I was grieved but I kept silence'.[3]

The sayings are usually short, practical and to the point. Generally speaking, the fathers do not indulge in theological speculation, but of course in any collection of sayings there is a theology implied, even if the underlying theme owes more to the editor than the original fathers.

But why go into the desert in the first place? Why should Christians in the late third and fourth century suddenly decide that the place to search for God is among the rocks and sand? Part of the answer is that the 'desert' in Christian and Jewish tradition is the place where God is found. The desert of Sinai was where the Israelites wandered for forty years, found their identity and learned what it was to be a pilgrim people. The desert of Judaea was where John the Baptist preached repentance, and Jesus was tempted for forty days. Even St Paul spent three years in the desert of Arabia after his conversion.

For the Jews and for the early Christians, the desert was the habitat of evil spirits. It was the place where later generations of monks would choose to go, in order to do battle with the forces of evil. When the opportunities for martyrdom were lacking, after the peace of Constantine, the desert was the place to go, to prove one's worth.

However, the deserts of Northern Egypt attracted many recluses even before Constantine. In North Africa, distance from the Mediterranean coast also meant distance from the rule of Roman law. In the desert there were outlaws, tax-exiles, thieves and vagabonds, as well as pagan and Christian 'holy men'. The old word for a desert hermit was 'anchorite', a word which simply means 'drop-out' or 'one who has withdrawn'.[4] The early desert fathers were perceived as 'drop-outs' from society and, to some degree, 'drop-outs' from the Church as well. We shall return to this last point at the end of the chapter. For the moment, it is enough to note that there was a long tradition in Egypt of journeying into the desert as a means of escape or protest.

Pagan ascetics and soothsayers made their dwellings in desert caves. It was the custom of the curious as well as the honest inquirers to go out from Alexandria and visit them to ask advice or to study their way of prayer. The Christian desert fathers fitted with some modification into this tradition. The idea of *apatheia*, freedom from all passions, which was so sought after by the stoic ascetics, quickly found its way into the vocabulary of the desert fathers too. The sayings of the fathers are full of examples of visitors from the towns or cities who come to ask their advice on prayer and self-discipline. Not so many decades before, they might have come out to the pagan holy men to ask their advice too. The wisdom of the pagans was gradually being eclipsed by the light of Christ.

It was taken for granted among the desert fathers that theirs was a celibate way of life. Following the example of Jesus and the apostles they were dedicated to celibacy for the sake of the Kingdom. Yet they are not presented as people who found this easy or free of difficulty and temptation. Athanasius tells in the *Life of Anthony* how Anthony had to struggle with his own sexual desires, as he had to struggle with so many other things. Two points are important here. The first is that the desert fathers are not presented as ready-made saints or paragons of virtue. They are *struggling* with their unruly natures, and are not always successful in the struggle. They are presented as travellers rather than people who have arrived.

Many sayings of the fathers tell of encounters which deal specifically with monks who have sinned.

> A brother whom another brother had wronged, came to see Abba Sisoes and said to him, 'My brother has hurt me and I want to avenge myself'. The old man pleaded with him, saying, 'No, my child, leave vengeance to God'. He said to him, 'I shall not rest until I have avenged myself'. The old man said, 'Let us pray, Brother'. Then the old man stood up and said, 'God, we no longer need you to care for us, since we can do justice for ourselves'. Hearing these words, the brother fell at the old man's feet, saying 'I will no longer seek justice from my brothers. Forgive me, Abba'.[5]

The second point is that the desert is not a quiet, tranquil place for rest and recuperation. It is more like the arena where combat takes place. Our modern (and not very healthy) presuppositions

41

about solitude, quiet and distance from city life tend to identify the desert with quiet and refreshing places of retreat and relaxation. This was not the desert of the desert fathers. Consider the following episode from the *Life of Anthony*:

> So the devil kept a close watch on Anthony and gnashed his teeth against him . . . but Anthony was heartened by the Saviour, remaining unharmed by the devil's villainy and subtle strategy. Thus he set wild beasts on him as he kept vigil in the night; and well-nigh all the hyenas in the desert came out of their lairs and encircled him. With him in their midst, each with open jaw threatened to bite him. But he, knowing well the enemy's craft, said to them all, 'If you have received the power to do this against me, I am ready to be devoured by you; if you have been sent by demons, get out without delay, for I am Christ's servant'. As Anthony was saying this, they fled, as though hounded by the whip of that word.[6]

Whatever the desert was for Anthony, it was *not* a place of quiet retreat! In the desert one confronted one's own weakness, and this was a *struggle* from beginning to end. More importantly, God was to be found not at the end of the struggle, but precisely in the middle of the fight.

The following story is told by Abba Elias:

> An old man was living in a temple and the demons came to say to him, 'Leave this place which belongs to us,' and the old man said 'No place belongs to you'. Then they began to scatter his palm leaves about, one by one, and the old man went on gathering them together with perseverance. A little later the devil took his hand and pulled him to the door. When the old man reached the door, he seized the lintel with the other hand, crying out, 'Jesus, save me'. Immediately the devil fled away. Then the old man began to weep. Then the Lord said to him, 'Why are you weeping?' and the old man said, 'Because the devils have dared to seize a man and treat him like this'. The Lord said to him. 'You had been careless. As soon as you turned to me again, you see I was beside you'.[7]

The lesson again is that the desert is not a quiet place of tranquillity but a place of struggle. The middle of the struggle, however, is precisely where God is to be found.

However, the desert fathers did not spend their entire day fighting demons. Most of their time was occupied by work and prayer. They had to grow or obtain their own food. Even the barren desert was capable of supporting simple agriculture, and many lived simply off the vegetables they grew themselves. Some would make mats or baskets from the reeds that grew near the Nile, and sell them to occasional visitors. They lived from the fruits of their own labours.

Their diet of prayer was mainly the Psalms, most of which would be known by heart. They prayed too by keeping silence, or repeating the name *Jesus* over and over again. Generally speaking their prayer was very simple and they represent a return to simplicity in prayer and ascetic practice. It is not to be wondered at that all the Psalms were frequently known by heart. Huge chunks of the New Testament were known by heart too. It was the age of the trained memory.

There is, among the desert fathers, a certain scepticism about the value of reading, and a bias towards learning by word of mouth and by memory. Athanasius, a very learned man himself, takes delight in describing his hero Anthony as illiterate. Perhaps here there is a reaction against the sophisticated philosophical and theological debates of the big cities. The desert fathers lived during a period of several important schisms and heresies, (e.g. the Meletians, the Donatists, the Arians, the Gnostics) and their anti-intellectual bias is a reaction against those who argue about Christian principles instead of living them.

> A brother said to Abba Serapion, 'Give me a word'. The old man said to him, 'What shall I say to you? You have taken the living of widows and orphans and put it on your shelves'. For he saw them full of books![8]

Books represented vanity, futility and wealth too.

It is the desert fathers' concern with the practical rather than the intellectual which gives rise to their most admired characteristic: a sense of compassion. Because they have a deep sense of their own sinfulness and the weakness of all humanity, a great sense of compassion for the weakness of others comes through many of their sayings. A story is told about Abba Ammonas, who was called upon by some monks to go with them to punish a local hermit who was thought to have a mistress living with him.

> When the hermit in question heard this, he hid the woman in a large cask. The crowd of monks came to the place. Now Abba Ammonas saw the position clearly, but for the sake of God he kept the secret; he entered, seated himself on the cask and commanded the cell to be searched. Then when the monks had searched everywhere without finding the

> woman, Abba Ammonas said, 'What is this? May God
> forgive you!' After praying, he made everyone go out, then
> taking the brother by the hand he said, 'Brother, be on your
> guard'. With these words he withdrew.[9]

What is evident here is Ammonas' reluctance to condemn, and
his willingness to show compassion with the weakness of others.
This is probably one of the most endearing characteristics of the
desert fathers. A similar story is told of Moses the Black.

> A brother at Scetis committed a fault. A council was called
> to which Abba Moses was invited, but he refused to go to
> it. Then the priest sent someone to say to him, 'Come, for
> everyone is waiting for you'. So he got up and went. He
> took a leaking jug, filled it with water and carried it with
> him. The others came out to meet him and said to him,
> 'What is this, Father?' The old man said to them 'My sins
> run out behind me and I do not see them, and today I am
> coming to judge the faults of another'. When they heard
> that, they said no more to the brother but forgave him.[10]

Again the compassionate approach triumphs over the
judgemental.

Abba Moses and Abba Ammonas were among that small
minority of desert fathers who were ordained — Moses as a priest,
and Ammonas as a bishop. Priests were actually rather scarce in
the Egyptian desert, and this simple fact raises two important
questions about desert spirituality. The first is about the eucharist,
and its seeming lack of importance in the thought of the desert
fathers. Few of the sayings of the fathers mention it, and whether
this silence is deliberate or accidental is impossible to know. In
an organised community like that of St Pachomius, or in some
of the *lavra*[11] communities, provision was made for the regular
community eucharist. But this was not universal. Sometimes the
eucharist would be celebrated when a visiting priest from
Alexandria came out to visit the hermits. But this could only have
been organised on a random or haphazard basis. It looks as
though many desert fathers of the early fourth century were not
particularly bothered by the absence of a regular eucharistic
celebration.

This leads us to the second question. The dearth of priests in
the desert communities may have been more than accidental. The
desert movement represents a protest not only against society
at large, but to some degree against ecclesiastical authority. This
is often attributed to the resentment felt at the prospect of priests
and bishops softening the demands of the Gospel and becoming

tools of the Roman Emperor, and there is some truth in this. But the trait was present even before the conversion of Constantine. Anthony became a desert hermit some forty-five years before Constantine.

The desert fathers do have a bias that is not only anti-intellectual but anti-clerical as well. Abba Pachomius once told his monks, 'The thought of ordination is the beginning of the love of command'.[12] Perhaps this echoes a feeling that Church authority was failing to inspire people, and that the only way Christian values could be lived was to get away not only from the temptations of the city, but from the Church of the city as well.

This explains St Athanasius' concern, in the *Life of St Anthony*, to stress Anthony's great respect for priests and bishops. Athanasius, writing about the year 358, in the middle of the Arian controversy, was anxious to enlist the support of the desert hermits out of town. As bishop of Alexandria, he had been ousted by the Arian party and on more than one occasion sought refuge with the desert hermits. This experience of opposition and exile must have helped him to grow in appreciation of the desert 'drop-outs', and he came to value their contribution to the life of the Church. He wrote of Anthony:

> Renowned man that he was, he yet showed the profoundest respect for the Church's ministry, and wanted every cleric to be honoured above himself. He was not ashamed to bow his head before bishops and priests; and if ever a deacon came to him for help, he conversed with him on what was helpful; but when it came to prayers, he would ask him to lead.[13]

Anthony's humility is here enlisted in support of Athanasius' own struggle against the Arian party in Alexandria. What is also occurring is an attempt to bring the desert protesters into a closer communion with the wider Church. Athanasius is part of a movement trying to draw the charismatic element into a more fruitful relationship with the institutional element. His stress on Anthony's obedience to bishops is not accidental.

Athanasius, having spent time in the desert with some of the monks, has come to realise that these strange anchorites have something to teach the Church of the city. But this is only possible if they remain part of the wider Church, and do not become a separate sect.

Perhaps it is here that the story of the desert fathers has most to teach us. This struggle between institution and inspiration has been echoed many times in the history of the Church. Sometimes it has been experienced very fruitfully, as with Innocent III's encouragement of St Francis and St Dominic. At other times the experience has been a tragic one, as with Urban VIII's suppression of Mary Ward's communities. What is certain, is that, in every age, the Church needs her prophetic witnesses, who will live in a creative way the demands of the Gospel.

The business of their integration within the wider communion of the Church can be more or less messy depending on the goodwill of 'prophets' and the openness of the rest of the Christian community, particularly its leaders. But to ignore the prophetic witness is in the end to betray the Gospel.

In modern times the relationship between the Church and her 'prophets' has not been a very happy one. This is partly due to the inherited fear of ideas that goes back to Reformation times, and which has become reinforced by a very 'private' spirituality. But is is also due to the sheer rapidity of the upheavals of the twentieth century. No century has ever seen such rapid change.

The political upheavals, the technological advances, and the social upheavals of the twentieth century have all played their part in making the job of a prophetic witness extremely difficult. When threatened with the upheavals caused by the microchip, modern weapons or mass poverty, the tendency to cling for security to what is familiar asserts itself among Christians, both lay and clerical. But it is precisely in this situation that prophetic witness is most sorely needed.

The desert fathers of the fourth century gave prophetic witness in an age of upheaval when a great empire was in decline. They stood apart from the values of Imperial Rome and, by their lives, recalled the Church to the values of the Gospel. Today we need the witness of their successors as never before.

4

Three medieval English mystics

by
David McLoughlin

The glories of twelfth and thirteenth century Church life were over. Christendom as an entity was on the decline. The fourteenth century Church did not look too good. Relations between England and the French Papacy were breaking down. Church discipline, especially among the clergy and hierarchy, left much to be desired. Theology had degenerated in great part to unreal, hair-splitting debates. Langland, in his *Piers Plowman*, described the decomposition brilliantly.

But in the midst of this break-up and decline, there were developments of a more positive nature. The national languages began to develop and a national literature emerges with works like Geoffrey Chaucer's wry commentaries on English life, *The Canterbury Tales*.

English had been the language of the uneducated; but in the fourteenth century it broke increasingly into polite society, and in great part, it was the women of the time who were the language's champions. While often educated, the nuns, anchoresses and pious dames spoke English and so their directors wrote for them in English. As a result, an expanding literature on the spiritual life emerged in English.

It was in this language of the people, which we call Middle English, that the English Mystics expressed themselves.

There are really only four figures of stature in the mystical writing of this period: Richard Rolle, the anonymous author of the *Cloud of Unknowing*, Mother Julian of Norwich, and Walter Hilton.

In this essay, I shall consider only the last three. While Richard Rolle was, of them all, the most popular spiritual writer of his time, his major works were in Latin, not English. Also there is a good reason to believe that Hilton and the *Cloud* author wrote, in part, to correct the imbalance caused by some interpretations of Rolle's teaching, in particular his emotive and colourful images.

The Cloud

The author of *The Cloud of Unknowing* is unknown. From his style of writing we can identify other books by him; the most important being the *Epistle of Privy Counsel*, the work of his maturity. He was a priest, a spiritual guide. He wrote the *Cloud* for young disciples, possibly to correct mistaken ideas they had picked up from others.

The ideas he draws on are not original. He belongs to a tradition stretching back to the writing of Dionysius, the sixth century Syrian monk whose thought has had almost as much influence on Christian spiritual writing as the Gospels. He translated Dionysius' most famous work, *Dionise Hid Divinite*. Terms he uses, like 'cloud of unknowing' and 'cloud of forgetting' can be found in the writings of the great twelfth-century French mystical theologian, Richard of St Victor. And terms like 'naked intent' and 'a naked wind without image' can be found in the writing of St Albert the Great. Despite this pedigree, the author is rather anti-intellectual. The universities were no longer what they had been at the time of St Albert; they were now rather decadent. Our author emphasises love, the will, rather than knowledge.

The Cloud of Unknowing is rambling in style — a sharing of wisdom. Like all such sharing, it tends to include related issues, wandering from, and returning to, the main argument. The style is of an extended letter of direction, to a young religious with specific difficulties in an already advanced prayer life. It is not like Hilton's *The Scale*, a whole map — rather a detailed survey of a particular area.

The author knows that what he is talking about is particular and nowhere suggests it is everyone's way to contemplation. He respects our individuality and the unpredictable nature of God's call. He has seen what happens when people get the wrong sort of spiritual advice and so he warns people off in his foreword:

> Whoever you are possessing this book, know that I charge you with a serious responsibility, to which I attach the sternest sanctions that the bonds of love can bear. . .

> You are not to read it, write or speak of it, nor allow another to do so, unless you really believe that he is a person, deeply committed to follow Christ perfectly. . .

> As for worldly gossips, flatterers, the scrupulous, talebearers, busybodies, and the hypercritical, I would just

as soon they never laid eyes on this book. I had no intention
of writing for them and prefer that they do not meddle with
it. This applies, also, to the merely curious, educated or not.
They may be good people by the standards of the active life,
but the book is not suited to their needs.[1]

The question he is addressing is how to discern the work of
the Spirit — especially when prayer has become dark and silent.
He gives advice about a form of active silence — what he calls
naked intent — which cannot be achieved by a method (like yoga)
because it is in part the gift of God. But we can *prepare* to receive
it and it is this preparation which he considers.

Before looking at his advice, perhaps it would help to outline
his view of the spiritual life in its four stages. He speaks of it as
Common, Special, Singular and Perfect. The first three stages
begin and end in this life, the last can begin here but is fulfilled
only in heaven. Common is life governed by the Commandments
and external sanctions, characterised by constraint and dread; it
involves no first-hand knowledge. Special is that stage when the
soul awakened to God responds in obedience and service. This
leads into the Singular stage where the soul is increasingly pre-
occupied with the love of God.

In the light of these stages, he categorises mankind as Active
or Contemplative. The first stage of Active life involves physical
works of mercy. The believer goes out from self to the other. The
second stage involves discursive prayer, increasingly entering into
oneself through meditation, compunction and praise, until the
first stage of the contemplative is reached, marked by thanks, by
learning and study. Stage 2 of the Contemplative life is the
entering of The Cloud of Unknowing, going beyond self — which
at least for a time demands that Stages 2 and 3 cease.

These are not exclusive stages since the Contemplative is never
freed from the demands of charity, and salvation is offered to
Active or Contemplative alike; we do not choose our state, God
calls us.

Now let us look more closely at his account of the move from
the Active to the Contemplative life. He speaks of two stages.
The first is the gradual freeing from dependence on people and
things. He calls this entering the Cloud of Forgetting. We must
enter a Cloud of Forgetting as regards others. But even if we
manage this we are still conscious of *self*:

> . . . a naked knowing, and feeling of your own being. . .[2]

This self-consciousness has to be dealt with before we can reach

> nothing but the union effected between God and the Soul
> in perfect love.[3]

To leave self-consciousness behind is to enter the Cloud of Unknowing — which is a naked intent directed to God alone. This is as far as Man can manage; the rest is of God.

How do we manage this forgetting and this unknowing? What about sin? What about thoughts and distractions, good or bad? He tells us: the fire of love/charity burns up the guilt. He takes Mary Magdalene as the example of the Contemplative attitude to sin. Because she loved much, her sin was forgiven. She did not grovel in the memory of her sin; all memories have to be trodden under the Cloud of Forgetting. How?

Firstly, like Mary Magdalene, concentrate on your desire for God; let that be your focus.

Secondly, instead of resisting evil thoughts, relax body, mind and imagination, aware of the presence of God. Realise your own helplessness before evil and allow God to work for you. Hilton gives the same advice.

They are suggesting an awareness exercise — focus on your desire for God, realise your helplessness and dependence, use the temptations, bad thoughts, etc., to help you realise your need all the more.

If this is practised, this contrition which focuses on our needs rather than on our sins, then the pain of actual sin will disappear. What remains is the awareness of original sin, of our fractured state, what he calls 'the lump of Sin', an awareness which reminds us of God's mercy and which provokes humility.

Out of this gradual realisation of our dependence on God, a deep, placid sorrow emerges. This sorrow forms the last stage of preparation for the gift of Contemplation. The aim of all this preparation is to arrive at a self-awareness which is a 'naked intent unto God'. It is a gradual purification of the will to love — until there is nothing between us and God:

> Knit to God in spirit, in oneness of love and union of wills.[4]

This is the Cloud of Unknowing. Walter Hilton speaks of the same state:

> Then the soul meditates on essential nothingness. For then it is meditating on one thing and clinging to it. This is a rich 'nothing', and this 'nothing' and this 'night' are a great vacation for the soul who desires the love of Jesus.[5]

Those who have experienced this prayer are drawn to it almost against their will. It seems useless, futile, the mind appears blank, thoughts impossible. No pious thoughts or resolutions arise. It can seem a foolish exercise, a waste of time.

What the author is saying is that human methods are human activities, whereas in passive prayer the action is Divine. *The Cloud* teaches a method of preparation (*noughting*) of God's intervention. It suggests the human response least likely to hinder God's work.

The author is trying to help his disciple to come before God as an infinite capacity, an empty space to be filled with the divine presence. He suggests we approach God in our naked being, as potential that God may give us definition, that we might become fully realised in him.

What prayer is appropriate to this preparation?

> The shorter the word the better, being more like the working of the Spirit.[6]

> . . . a short prayer pierces heaven.[7]

Short acclamations: God, Lord, *Abba*, are best suited to this naked intent of the soul. They cause the minimum interference between God and the soul. But they must be rich, full words, 'secretly meant in the depths of the spirit'.

They represent our desire, the soul's intent, breaking into word. He compares them to the shout of 'Fire' — all the fear, horror, warning, concern, helplessness of that shout in a medieval town where the houses were little more than wattle and daub and whole streets could be aflame in seconds. Such words then are *foci* for our naked intent. They draw it to a point.

This state of 'unknowing' places nothing between God and us. Prayer then becomes a being in the present eternal act of God's life.

We are to enter and live out of the life of God.

The whole thrust of the author's thought is an attempt to avoid the pride of the intellectual believer, who thinks if you give him space, time and a method, he will find God. He is suspicious of methods and emphasises that any spiritual way is a preparation for what only God can give.

Yet at the same time, with his idea of 'naked intent' he wishes to avoid the empty-headed 'spiritual' who imagines that by becoming vacuous he has arrived. He is only too aware that the spirit which fills such emptiness is not necessarily the Holy Spirit.

To avoid these extremes, he emphasises that all this should take place within the ordinariness of Church life, of Church authority, sacramental life, obedience to the law of charity, attentiveness to the Scriptures. He emphasises the need for a prudent confessor, the need to be attuned to an open and healthy conscience. For him the heights of contemplation rest on a simple and sure foundation, the life of the Church.

This emphasis on our need for the Church's help is common to all the English Mystics and, in particular, to Julian of Norwich whose *Shewings*, or *Revelations of Divine Love*, I would like to consider next.

Julian of Norwich

On 8 May 1371, the thirty-one-year-old Julian, while apparently dying in her little cell attached to the church, received fifteen revelations and on the following night she received a sixteenth revelation. These were written down shortly afterwards; then twenty years later she wrote her explanation and commentary upon them.

She had been a nun since she was a young woman but these visions seem to have been her first mystical experience. Her initial response was to think of them as the fruit of her illness: 'I said I had raved'.[8]

She is in bed, thought to be dying, already paralysed from the waist down. By the time the priest arrives she is speechless, then her sight fades until all she can see is the cross the priest holds before her face. Paralysis spreads upwards until she can scarcely breathe. Then suddenly all pain ceases and the visions begin, lasting some five hours. When they end, pain returns, paralysis ceases; she falls asleep and receives a further vision in a dream.

It has been suggested that the whole thing smacks of acute neurosis, perhaps the result of over-enthusiastic penance and too much solitude. However, no-one present thought that Julian was raving; in fact, they laughed when she suggested it and their laughter ceased the moment she began to speak of the content of her visions.

It seems, like others before her and since, Julian had set out on the quest for God young, full of holy desires, willing to die to the world for the sake of her Lover. These desires needed purifying, re-ordering.

The beginning of that final purification seems to have come with her sickness and her revelations. Such revelations have sometimes marked the beginning of real progress in the lives of other saints, e.g., Catherine, Bernadette. But with Julian the purification lasted longer, twenty years longer. Only then did she feel she understood them.

Then she becomes conscious that her message, the meaning of her experience, is for 'every Christian'. It turns her outwards; she is to comfort and encourage the rest of us. This pattern is typical of the lives of the mystics: union with God, possession of God alone growing into possessing all things in God, and so in God moving out to all again.

Julian's central message is simple and comforting: 'All will be well'.[9]

God's abiding, sustaining love is her theme. She sees the whole of creation supported in the power of God the Father.

> He showed me something small, no bigger than a hazelnut, lying in the palm of my hand, as it seemed to me, and it was as round as a ball. I looked at it with the eye of my understanding and thought: What can this be? I was amazed that it could last, for I thought that because of its littleness it would suddenly have fallen into nothing. And I was answered in my understanding: It lasts and always will, because God loves it; and thus everything has being through the love of God.[10]

Everything exists only because God, making it, loves it and, loving it, preserves it from ceasing to exist. The comfort she offers is the vision of God as Creator and Conserver, the same theme as Michelangelo's Sistine Ceiling and the statuary on the front of Chartres Cathedral.

But how can we reconcile this with its seeming opposite, sin and the disintegrating power of evil? Julian does this by asking: 'What is sin?' For her sin is 'no need'. Evil is not a principle of power but rather a disorder. In the Revelation she sees:

> In this naked word 'sin', Our Lord brought generally to my mind all which is not good, and the shameful contempt and the direst tribulation which he endured for us in this life, and his death and all his pains, and the passions, spiritual and bodily, of all his creatures. . . And yet this was shown to me in an instant, and it quickly turned into consolation. For our good lord would not have the soul frightened by this ugly sight.[11]

There is no acceptance of evil as some equivalent power which can disturb God's providence. She almost dismisses evil. It is a nothing.

> . . .I believe that it has no kind of substance, no share in being, nor can it be recognised except by the pains which it causes.[12]

This is quite different from the popular religiosity of her time which tended to emphasise the power of evil and God's anger with sinners.

Julian's vision is of the changeless love of God. '. . .It is the most impossible thing which could be that God might be angry'.[13]

God cannot be angry. Since we exist by his will, if he were truly angry, we would cease to exist. Rather there is no distinction between God's will and his love. It is the evil man who perceives God's love as wrath; God does not change. This theme of the abiding love of God is the heart of her message.

What is fascinating is the authority of her simple statements. She sees all true mysticism as born and derived from the first simple act of faith, in which a man submits himself to the Word of God.

This act of believing, eventually, through the work of the Holy Spirit, becomes more passive and receptive. But it is not something qualitatively different. Anything that happens later is potential in that initial act of faith. So all of us, in Julian's eyes, are potential mystics from our first act of faith. And so Julian writes for all of us. We each share one vocation, the call to life with God, the only thing outside this vocation is sin.

We are called to a spiritual childhood which Julian develops around the idea of the motherhood of the second Person of the Trinity. The Word of God is the source of all that is made. It is the womb constantly nourishing, constantly bearing.

In the incarnation, the Word became flesh in the God-man, and raised human nature into God. United with the word we are taken into the life of God. We are conceived and born into the life of grace.

God is then both our Mother and Father, embracing in his/her love all the moment-to-moment details of our life. The highest state of prayer, the greatest fulfilment of God's call to holiness, is a child's simplicity, receiving sustenance from the divine womb, waiting on God from moment to moment.

The whole of life, then, for Julian is a becoming acclimatised to God. Growing in union in simple trust, helped by Mother Church which is one with her Lord. And as we grow in trust in the Lord's love, then gradually all is seen through God's love.

So I was taught that love is Our Lord's meaning.[14]

So Julian's teaching is essentially a simple one for all believers, a call to follow through the dynamic inherent within our initial act of faith. We are called to follow the path into the maternal love of God that is all embracing and against which sin and evil cannot prevail. Before it they are nothing; in fact they are non-life, non-being and the way to death and nothingness.

Walter Hilton

The third of our writers is Walter Hilton, an Augustinian Canon of Thurgarton, who died in 1395, some twenty years before Dame Julian. His most famous work, *The Stairway* or *Ladder of Perfection*, is written ostensibly for a woman 'closed in a house', for an anchoress like Julian. But he wrote aware of all those who try to love and serve God in this life and the next. His concern then is the whole of the spiritual life.

He reflects with sure judgement on the soul's way to God. His canvas is broad and generously proportioned, his language direct. There is nothing of the nit-picking of later Scholastic Mystical Theology. His language is lucid, sober and authoritative. He was a man of wide learning but also wide experience as a director of contemplatives. The structure of his writings is like a spiral staircase; as you mount higher you look back on your previous place, but now from a different angle, a different perspective. What has gone before is not forgotten or abandoned, but rather integrated into an ever new personal synthesis.

There is a delightful balance and sanity in his work. Unlike the author of the *Cloud*, he is not suspicious of the intellect but emphasises both knowledge *and* charity. There is no elitism here. All the baptised are in a state of grace, however busy, however marked by venial sin. All of us are within the active power of charity, of God's love moving us to perfect love. Like Julian he is an optimist. Anyone responding to the grace of the present can be led forward by the love of God to contemplation and gradual transformation into Christ.

He sees this process as revealing the true image of Christ in the soul. The Word made flesh, Jesus, is the true mirror in which we can see our true nature within the trinitarian life of God.

The shadow of sin has dimmed the true image and so we tend to create our own unholy trinity. Turning in on ourself we become the measure of ourselves; just as the measure of the Father is the Son his Word, so the sinner's word is self, not the word spoken by the Father, but a self-reflection turned in on self in pride.

Pre-occupied with self, measuring the world in terms of self, the sinner 'breathes forth' himself. His will is increasingly self-orientated with all sorts of evil consequences. So the sinner, his word and his will form an unholy trinity. Mind and will feed on self rather than God. But this self is a nothing, an emptiness.

Hilton realises that this unholy circle cannot be broken at once. A gradual transformation is required. But the tendency to sin, which is sadly now part of us, Hilton sees as an occasion of grace. Each vice can become, through God's grace, a virtue.

Stubbornness can become fortitude; selfish desire can be transformed into singleness of purpose, and so on. Before the incarnate Word, our sinfulness makes us humble, malleable, aware of our need of God. Temptations, even falls, remain but Hilton says 'don't dwell on them'. Get a good director so you don't become base, but then get cracking on the way; the way which is the stairway of perfection.

Allow your focus to shift from self and sin to God. Use the means available, the Sacraments, to encounter Christ. These early steps, from our sinful self-image to the discovery of the image of Christ, take place in the normal sacramental life of the Church which is available to all believers. It is precisely in the everyday sacramental life of the Church that the living word of God, our true image, is to be found.

Hilton is always a man of the Church. He rejoices in its tradition and wisdom, a collective mind and will so much richer than our own limited experience. He sees Church life as a source of strength, especially in the early stages of struggle with self:

> for Holy Church, who is the Mother of all these souls and has a tender love for all her children, prays spiritually for them and asks everything for them tenderly from her spouse, who is Jesus. She obtains for them health of soul by virtue of his passion, especially for those who cannot speak for themselves. . .[15]

Hilton is suspicious of feelings. In this he is reacting against writers like Rolle who seem to focus on bodily sensation. He recalls that Our Lord told his disciples it was 'speedful' that he leave them because they were too bound to his humanity, to Jesus of Nazareth, whereas in the Spirit they were called to follow the Risen Christ. Focusing exclusively on Jesus of Nazareth can prevent the further revelation of the God that we are called to know, the God who is Father, Son and Spirit.

Warm feelings, consolations as they are sometimes called, will come and go. Rejoice in them when they come but do not yearn for them. It may be we are being called to move beyond them. Hilton does not despise feelings but he does not place too much trust in them. He believes we are ultimately called beyond affection and knowledge to a purer love of God characterised by wisdom and understanding, a love independent of imagination or emotion, what he calls 'a restful darkness' (*II-29*); a state free from reliance on devotion, less obviously enthusiastic, less seeming-pious, less demonstrative. In fact, the believer in this state could almost pass for one who hardly knows prayer and its joys.

This reforming or purifying of experience leads to such union with God that we take on the image of the Son and enter into Jesus' relationship to the Father.

> For these souls who bear the complete image and likeness of His Son Jesus are particularly His own sons.[16]

All that is required of us in all this is a desire for God.

> . . . for prayer is nothing else but the desire of the heart rising to God by being withdrawn from all earthly thoughts.[17]

To put God first is to be already at prayer. Then the Lord is already present in our minds and will. There may be a long way ahead, much evil to be countered and disposed of, yet we are already held in the goodness of God. Hilton has wonderful confidence in man's capacity for God and God's desire for man. This is confidence based not on a hollow optimism but on long experience as a confessor and guide.

Two forms of prayer are particularly helpful to begin with and are the appropriate expression of the believer's desire for God.

The first is the prayer of the Church; the Liturgy and especially the Office:

> By this prayer the soul of a flesh-governed man, who is always falling downward into worldly thoughts and fleshy affections, will be lifted up from them and will be held up as by a staff.[18]

Liturgical prayer undergirds the developing life of the believer, providing appropriate 'food'.

The second form is to pray short, simple phrases, perhaps from the Scriptures. These form a response to the gift of knowing and experiencing God's love. Hilton speaks of this as a burning fire of the heart which lasts only a while, since we could not bear it long. But while it does not last long, its influence remains, enabling us to lead a more faithful life.

The two forms of prayer lead to a third, it

> emerges from the heart alone, without words. It comes with great rest and comfort of body and soul. Whoever would pray well in this manner must have a clean heart.[19]

This prayer of rest is the fruit of much active prayer and penance. It becomes an habitual state of prayer, enabling a continuous love and praise of God. But distractions, especially desire for things other than God, can still impinge and disturb this prayer of rest. Hilton's advice is simply 'don't worry, just continue to attend as well as you can'.

For Hilton, then, the underlying dynamic of all growth in prayer is the desire for God. The actual reformation or purifying of faith and feeling takes time. But from the start it is never simply our work. Prayer is always already the fruit of grace with which we cooperate. At some point in our growth this dependence on God's grace will become more clear. We will pass through a period of darkness. Then our motives must become purified. Then it will become clear that our growth rests in God and is not something we can achieve alone.

Hilton speaks of this darkness as a 'good night'. Then we realise our own nothingness, our inability to pray unless Christ prays with us. The desire for God becomes more urgent, more painful, as we realise we can do nothing further ourselves.

In talking of this process, Hilton speaks of a night of purification between two days. The first day is lit by the light of the world's loveliness. Our thoughts and affections have to be freed from this if we are to appreciate the light of the second day, which is the love of Christ in which we gain true freedom.

The early part of the night, the early stages of detachment, are painful. But like the night, it passes; we cannot hurry it, as any insomniac knows, so there is no point in straining.

> . . . and don't strive too much . . . you must wait for grace and endure patiently. Don't tear yourself apart too much, but if you can, gently draw your desire and your spiritual attention to Jesus. . . .[20]

The darker the night gets, the nearer is the dawn. A positive purification begins, a greater awareness of the glory coming, of the presence of Jesus; desire for the Lord increases. Darkness is complete. The senses cease to clamour for the old life, the heart is at rest, waiting. There are no dreams, no movement, just the rise and fall of breath. Breathing unknowingly, without thoughts, the love of God.

> This is a rich 'nothing' and this 'nothing' and this 'night' are a great vacation for the soul who desires the love of Jesus.[21]

The risen Jesus, close throughout, now draws closer as the distractions of the first day recede. The second day begins to dawn and with it:

> . . . the true light of spiritual knowledge shall dawn within you — not all at once, but, secretly, little by little.[22]

The loveliness of Christ dawns on the believer, the light of an unseeable but real presence beyond image and description. In this darkness of the imagination and reason:

> . . . the soul experiences in understanding something of that thing which it had before in naked belief — and that is the beginning of contemplation.[23]

With the dawning of the new day, the formed love of the creature, the fruit of grace and nature, is transformed by the pure unformed love of God himself, the activity of the Holy Spirit.

Words are no longer appropriate. They were fine during the period of wooing, of engagement, but now the soul is wed. Love is both given and received. The two loves become one. Our restless seeking heart is stilled, we leave aside doing, saying, praying, and listen to the word that is not spoken.

The wonderful thing about Hilton's writing is his realism. The soul which has entered the life of God like this does not leave the rest of life behind. But now that life and especially the Gospels, Office and Mass take on different emphasis. Initially they were the expression of our desire for God; now that desire has been filled by the Spirit's coming. Gospels, Office, Mass are gathered into a unified vision in Christ, seen now not from outside but from within.

The process of dying to the world has led to the regaining of all of it from within an understanding of God's love — in this way, Walter Hilton describes the way to God.

The writings of these three authors are based on personal experience. They speak with a spiritual authority rarely equalled in the literature of our country. They reflect a stream of English Christianity never quite lost but often overshadowed. They speak to us today, in blunt clear language, as strongly as ever they did to English men and women of their time.

5

The *Imitation of Christ*

by
Peter Lawlor

We shall consider now a book which could not be omitted from any list of classical Christian writing. The earliest complete manuscript which has survived is of 1427; and in another forty years the book was known and loved all over Europe. This immediate success became permanent. Its appeal has been felt by all Christians, not only by Catholics. Furthermore, this remarkable popularity is even greater recommendation in view of the uncompromising nature of the work. In *The Tablet* for 20 April, 1940, Ronald Knox wrote as follows about the *Imitation*:

> The whole work was meant to be, surely, what it is — a sustained irritant which will preserve us if it is read faithfully from sinking back into relaxation: from self-conceit, self-pity, self-love. It offers consolation here and there, but always at the price of fresh exertion, of keeping your head pointing up-stream. Heaven help us if we find easy reading in the 'Imitation of Christ'. If a man tells you that he is fond of the 'Imitation', view him with sudden suspicion; he is either a dabbler or a saint.

Yet in spite of its forthright demands, it has earned the loyalty of most strangely assorted people. In the sixteenth century, St Ignatius called it the pearl of books; this perhaps is hardly surprising but it is unexpected to discover that in the nineteenth century Comte, the founder of modern positivism, read a chapter of the *Imitation* daily for many years before his death. Further in praise of it, George Eliot wrote as follows:

> . . .turning bitter waters into sweetness. . . a lasting record of human needs and human consolations; the voice of a brother who, ages ago, felt and suffered and renounced — in the cloister, perhaps, with serge gown and tonsured head,

with much chanting and long fasts and with a fashion of speech different from ours — but under the same, silent, far-off heavens, and with the same passionate desires, the same failures, the same weariness.

Perhaps George Eliot has put her finger on the reason for the book's enduring appeal. It is a perceptive expression of each man's struggle with himself. For all these reasons, Ronald Knox was devoted to the work, made a practice of reading a daily chapter for many years before his death and left unfinished a translation he had been making.

The necessity to assess historical context is not limited to sacred scripture. No book can properly be understood in divorce from its background.

Thomas à Kempis lived from 1380 to 1471. The background to all his spirituality was the movement known as the *Devotio Moderna*. It was modern, or new, in the sense that it became influential after nearly a century and a half dominated by the Friars. The *Devotio Moderna* originated in Holland and its founder was Gerard Groote (1340-1384). He was a man of considerable education who had led a worldly life until, at the age of thirty-five, he was converted through his friendship with Ruysbroeck. In the later part of his life, Gerard gathered round himself a group which in 1381 became the 'Brotherhood of the Common Life'. The brothers founded schools and many famous people were to come under their influence — Thomas à Kempis, Nicholas of Cusa, Erasmus and, indeed, Luther.

At first, the brothers were not bound by any vows, but they met together for prayer and gave their lives to the copying of religious books. Some of the brethren made a new foundation at Windesheim and then this group became religious in the technical sense. They became Canons Regular of the Augustinian rule. The best known member of this community was Thomas of Kempen. (Kempen is a small town near Cologne.) There is now a fairly general consensus among scholars that Thomas à Kempis is the author of *Imitation* though the authorship has been disputed, particularly in the seventeenth century.[1] It is perhaps of interest that the present title, *Imitation of Christ*, is hardly correct. It is derived from the first words of the heading to the first chapter. This is in accordance with medieval custom. Each book has a separate title. These different titles show that there is no necessary order for the four books of the *Imitation*. Many editions, in fact, put the fourth book before the third. The whole work is thought by many scholars to have been the combination of four treatises which originally were independent.

With this in mind, we may make a brief analysis of the contents. Book 1 is mainly concerned with the reformation of character but already with an eye to higher things. Thus in Chapter 2: 'If we were thoroughly dead to ourselves and free from attachments within, we should be able to relish divine things and to have some experience of heavenly contemplation'.

Book 2 has to do with the establishment of Christ's reign in the soul by the killing of all self-love. Thus in Chapter 2: 'You are not to think that you have made any progress until you feel that you are everybody's inferior'. And in Chapter 2: 'One thing is still wanting . . . That a man should leave all and leave himself and go out of himself altogether and keep nothing of himself of self-love'. This book culminates in the famous uncompromising chapter 12 about the necessity of suffering.

Book 3 is still mainly occupied with the self-discipline which must be exercised if the soul is to be open to God.

Book 4 is a treatise on the Eucharist.

At this point, some critique of the work as a whole must be attempted. An assessment of the influence exerted by environment is necessary, as is now universally accepted, in the interpretation of the Bible. If this factor is neglected in the case of non-inspired writing, misunderstanding is inevitable. To take this factor into account is not to adopt an attitude which is critical in any bad sense of the word. But I think there has been a tendency to regard the *Imitation* out of all relation to its historical context, as a guide necessarily relevant to every situation. It seems that this entirely uncritical approach overlooks two important considerations.

Firstly, the *Imitation* was the product of a movement which was consciously in reaction against the abuse of speculative theology; and reactions, commonly, have a way of swinging too far in an opposite direction.

Secondly, the work is monastic in origin.

Let us take these two considerations in turn.

Firstly, the main consequence of the reaction against the abuse of speculative theology was that devotion bears little relation to dogma. Leaving aside the eucharistic treatise, this must account, I think, in large measure for its universal appeal. It is, in the modern sense, largely undenominational. Now, obviously Thomas à Kempis was not indifferent to Catholic dogma, still less hostile to it. But he was in violent reaction against the excesses of a speculative theology. The greatest figure in this speculative movement had been Eckhart and, whatever one thinks about his orthodoxy, it must be stated that his writing was extremely obscure.[2] Such a school of spirituality was open to abuse and self-deception and these unfortunate results did sometimes accompany the good results. There were, therefore, real abuses against which the brothers of the common life had every right to protest. But to protest against the abuse of speculative thought is one thing; to protest against speculative thought is another.

Gerard Groote certainly seems to have gone beyond a protest about abuses:

> Do not spend thy time in the study of geometry, arithmetic, rhetoric, dialectic, grammar, songs, poetry, legal matters or astrology; for all these things are reproved by Seneca and a good man should withdraw his mind's eye therefrom and despise them; how much more therefore should they be avoided by a spiritually minded man and a Christian . . . the purpose of a degree is either gain or preferment or vain glorification or worldly honour.

He also remarks that only the carnal-minded could be happy in a university — which is, I suppose, by any standards, going a bit far.

Nearly a century later, another member of the movement, John Wessel, was still taking a dim view of higher educaton. He wrote:

> There is a strong and weighty argument against universities to be drawn from the fact that Paul secured but little fruit at Athens, accomplishing more in the neighbouring city of Corinth and in Thessaly, which was then almost barbarous, than in the Attic city, at that time the fountain of Greek philosophy. It goes to show that liberal studies are not very pleasing to God.

Wessel was a friend of Thomas à Kempis and this background of excessive reaction makes it easier to see certain famous passages of the *Imitation* as part of an historical pattern. It must be stated that there is a sentence in the *Imitation* which puts a brake on some of the wilder statements of Groote and Wessel. (*Book 1. Ch. 3*) 'No reason why we should quarrel with learning or with any straightforward pursuit of knowledge; it is all good as far as it goes and part of God's plan.' But, 'always what we should prize most is a clear conscience and holiness of life'. Now the truth of this latter remark no one will dispute. Nor will many dispute that academic characters need frequent exhortation lest they come, in Newman's phrase, 'to prefer intellectual excellence to moral'.

What I suggest we need to think about is another question: whether the *Imitation's* exposition of this theme, heavily weighted as it is by the outlook of the author's religious community, may not, if it goes unqualified, have harmful effects. Now it does seem that there is more here than the simple statement that virtue is more important than knowledge. Several passages seem to suggest at least an opposition between virtue and learning — which is a different matter from a statement of their relative importance.

It would be easy to contrast these passages from the *Imitation* with the writing of many authorities. Suffice it to say that the following passage from St Francis de Sales is quoted with emphatic approval by Pius XI in his encyclical on the priesthood:

> Priests who occupy themselves with works that hinder them from study are like men who refuse their stomach the food it needs for nourishment . . . ignorance in priests is more to be feared than sin . . . knowledge in priests is the eighth sacrament of the ecclesiastical hierarchy; and the Church's greatest misfortunes have come from this that the ark of knowledge has passed from the Levites into the keeping of others. If Geneva has wrought such terrible havoc among us, it is because, in our idleness, we did no more than read our breviaries without any care to make ourselves more learned.

As I said, this very strong passage is quoted by Pius XI. It seems to me the happy mean between à Kempis's 'Wherefore should we be anxious about genera and species?' and Cajetan's alleged assertion that any Dominican who spent less than four hours a day in study was guilty of mortal sin.

St Thomas Aquinas[3] has an article which is relevant here. He asks 'whether a religious order ought to be founded for the purpose of study?' He argues for the usefulness of study to religious who are contemplatives: 'It enlightens their minds', he says, and removes errors 'which frequently happen in the contemplation of things divine to those who are ignorant of the Scriptures. If the order is one whose mission is to preach, the need of study is evident. But, for all, study is a most valuable ascetic aid. The hard work of study tames the insubordination of sexual instinct, takes away the lust for riches and is a means to learn obedience.'

St Thomas seems rather to have narrowed the horizons here and I think we should close these reflections by looking to something of fundamental and universal importance. Namely, that it is clearly the mind of the Church that Christian life and prayer should be built upon the central themes of God's Revelation: the great biblical themes of Trinity, Incarnation and Redemption.

Without study, regarded as a matter of great importance, these themes will be remote from thinking, preaching and, therefore, Christian life. Certainly, they could not be gained from the *Imitation* alone. Ronald Knox, for all his love of the work, remarks that the very existence of the Holy Spirit is only recognised in one or two stray allusions. So what I am suggesting is simply this: that while the *Imitation* has a great deal to offer and has earned its abiding place in Christian literature, it is not all-sufficient. To disregard its historical context would be misleading in a serious way.

One main source of misunderstanding could be this: if devotion tends to become divorced from dogma, it inevitably tends to become excessively individualistic for it tends to move away from God's revealed plan of salvation which is a social one. Private prayer can then move far away from the mind of the Church as manifested in, say, the Easter Vigil. There need be no opposition between the individual and the community; it is only that both must be kept in view if Catholic life is to be lived in its fullness. Certainly each has his own soul to save and there is a personal responsibility here. But this self which has to be saved is a member of a Body, a branch of a Vine. The salvation of the individual Christian is the eternal safeguarding of his place within the Whole Christ. Whether this is adverted to or not, that is the meaning of individual salvation and so our efforts towards salvation should conform to the reality of God's plan.

The *Imitation's* monastic origin was the second consideration I mentioned. I meant by this only that the environment of contemplative life, coupled with the individualistic tendency just mentioned, has produced counsels which would not appear to be of universal validity; e.g. Book 1: 'Keep your friendship for God and His holy angels, shunning the acquaintance of men'. And 'What does the old tag say? I never yet went out among men, without feeling less of a man when I came home'. 'How often we have that experience at the end of a long chat. Easier to keep your mouth shut than to talk without saying too much; easier to bury yourself away at home than to watch your step successfully in public. If you are really aiming at an interior life, a spiritual life, you must be with Jesus, away from the crowd.'

Clearly, for one with a vocation to the monastic life, this could be sound advice — and this was the context of its giving. It surely needs qualification when addressed to one who has found his vocation in Our Lord's prayer at the Last Supper: 'I am not asking that thou shouldst take them out of the world but only that thou shouldst keep them from the evil one' (*John 17:15*).

In conclusion then, I suggest for your consideration that the

Imitation of Christ by à Kempis is one of the great books of Christian spirituality. It has earned its place in the affections of widely various people. There is vast profit to be gained from the constant perusal of its uncompromising realism. It has all the tonic effects of a cold shower, chief among which, I suppose, is the suppression of any tendency towards wishful thinking and self-deception. All this is true but a cautionary note needs to be sounded. The book should not be taken as a complete guide universally applicable to every situation; this would be to forget its historical setting. It would be, I think, to endanger something very fundamental, the relevance of dogma to devotion. This danger can be avoided if the book is read with the qualification I have indicated in mind; so there are emphases to be balanced up and lacunae to be filled.

6

Without a shadow of compromise: the unlovable mystic, St John of the Cross

by
Mervyn Tower

Allison Peers, without doubt the greatest English scholar, translator and editor of the works of John, claimed in his famous Reid Lecture in 1932 that John had been, until then, misrepresented as being dry, ascetic and morbid; and Allison Peers attempts to rehabilitate his character and flesh him out as a more normal, identifiable human being. He complains that John has been regarded as 'a prodigy of asceticism who lived in a world of his own and wrote not so much mystical as misty treatises which the ordinary mortal can be expected neither to understand nor to even read'.[1] Allison Peers expressed his hopes that John would come alive 'as one of the most attractive, invigorating and inspiring religious writers who ever lived'.[2]

To a certain extent, the vision of Allison Peers for John has blossomed in the sense of the number of publications and commentaries, in all languages, that have occurred since the 1930s. There has grown up a special adjective in Spanish to cope with such an input — *sanjuanista*. Yet despite this plethora and with the greatest respect for Allison Peers, John remains an uncomfortable, unattractive and unpalatable figure. Especially to a generation that still fundamentally demands and deserves the joyful welcoming, hospitable and communitarian aspect of the Faith, John certainly is initially unattractive, physically, in his alien, ascetic life-style, and in his relationship with and treatment of others.

Physically, he seems to have been attractive merely to a few nuns and bizarre women whose judgement one might legitimately doubt. There are no genuine portraits of John, but semi-contemporary portraits in pen show him to have small, grave features with a high forehead and deep-cut black eyes. The description of von Hugel of John as a 'massively virile contemplative' was not a record of his physical height which from skeletal examination is considered to have been about 4' 10". St Teresa, commenting not only on his learning but also on his stature, used to call him her *Senequita*.

However, a study of portraits and of death-masks of other Counter-Reformation saints reveals that physical attractiveness was not their common feature; and I am not claiming contrary to all evangelical and Christian tradition that physical looks are important. But the fact remains that, unlike so many of his contemporaries in holiness, there are few records of John being anything other than very austere with himself and with others. The light-relief in the catalogue of austerities is very sparse and there are no records of him displaying a sense of humour. Of course, there are many years of his life when we have little or no information about him — perhaps during these years he showed a different character. It **is** possible, but it would cut against the grain of someone who three years after becoming a Carmelite friar at the age of twenty-two wanted to become a Carthusian; and when persuaded not to by Teresa spent the remainder of his life imposing severe reform and discipline on his own Order as he, along with Teresa, nurtured the growth of the Discalced Carmelites.

Incident after incident paints John as uncompromising and severe though there is no doubt, as his letters for example witness, that he was quick to recognise the lunatic elements of excessive asceticism, of which there was no lack in sixteenth-century Spain.[3] John does blend, even more perhaps than Teresa, into his background: one is reminded of John's sovereign, the sombre Philip II, whose life was an endless series of mourning and funeral cortèges; of the restrictive and oppressive Inquisition with which John had a few brushes; of John's contemporary, the artist El Greco and his haunting madmen; and of another contemporary, the musician and composer Tomas Luis de Vittoria with his shrill, if beautiful, pathos. One is reminded of the morbid splendour of the Escorial with its large mausoleum — which John probably saw being built — especially given his interest in architecture and masonry.

This is the world of John of the Cross: Castile where he was born and grew up, the *tiera de cantos y santos*, the land of boulders and saints. His childhood was difficult; his study, both with the Jesuits and at Salamanca, scholastic and intense; his first years as a friar desperately severe. At Duruello, the first reformed

Carmelite priory, his cell was so low that he could only sit or lie down, and it was entered on hands and knees. The entrance hall of this converted wheat-store had been transformed into a chapel which Teresa tells us was covered with crosses and skulls. John slept with a stone for his pillow with more skulls littered around him. Teresa herself baulked at these conditions and told John he ought not to go barefoot in winter.[4] At times his severity and single-minded purposes, which he retained in all the posts he held and while he was travelling around, annoyed Teresa, causing her to remark rather cynically about him:

> God deliver us from people who are so spiritual they want to turn everything into perfect contemplation.[5]

In many ways the least ascetic, and seemingly the most human and normal event in John's life was his wanting to, his consenting to and his actual escape from prison in Toledo. Admittedly his offence was not a real one since he was accused of being a Discalced Carmelite; his prison sentence was the result of jealousy and the conditions of the prison were appalling. Yet such an act of conspiring to escape and actually escaping does seem to alleviate the litany of austerity and of penance; and I would venture to suggest that for a brief moment we glimpse a side of John that is possible to identify with — that of a broken, demoralised man, and we sympathise with him as he ate pears stewed in cinnamon while he recounted his prison-experience to the discalced sisters in Toledo with whom he found refuge.

Physically unattractive, given to severe asceticism, it was difficult for the person encountering him to warm to him. Austere with himself, the austerity continued in his relationship with and treatment of others. It seems to be true that he once rattled his rosary beads very loudly and coughed in order to cover up the illegal whispering of two novices who would have been punished for misdemeanour by their prior if found out; it is also true that John retained throughout his life a special relationship with the sick, and is reported to have ordered the best meats and wines once for some sick novices. But he seems to have found it painful to relate to people, except perhaps his brother Francesco de Yepes, on any level other than strict spiritual direction. When Teresa once told him in Confession that the affections she felt for him had affected her formal attitude of respect for him as a friar and priest, he snapped at her in no uncertain terms. Teresa certainly found him difficult and awkward at times and periodically became irritated by his attitude (*He* further went out of his way to aggravate *her* on occasions, such as when he purposely gave her a very small host at Mass knowing that she liked big ones).

Outside spiritual direction, John preferred to walk away and eat on his own his meagre lunches, rather than have to sit with strangers and make idle conversation. There is further little doubt that he continually made enemies by his actions and works and not merely in the Calced part of the Order. He himself seems to have retained likes and dislikes. Towards the last decade of his life he positively disliked his rectorship of the College at Baeza, not only because he did not enjoy the work, but also because, as he wrote to Teresa, he could not endure the frivolity of the people of Andalucia.[6]

It would not be inaccurate to say that contemporaries found it difficult to warm to him and remained awkward when with him. I believe this remains true today for most Christians. Abbot Chapman voices a reaction that was not just an initial one: 'For fifteen years or so, I hated St John of the Cross and called him a Buddhist'.[7] Yet, as I hope we shall see, John's unpalatable nature is above all the result of his maturity and faithfulness to ideals and of authenticity in reflecting in all circumstances and to all people the central characteristics of the interior life.

The question to be asked, of course, is not how such a difficult and unattractive character became a saint (friendliness and positive virtues of hospitality have never been major criteria for sanctity), but why Pius XI in 1926 could voice officially the feeling of the universal Church and declare him the Mystical Doctor.

Doctor Misticus. What is it about John that makes him an absolutely essential ingredient to any course on spirituality worthy of the name? We must answer this question in two ways: firstly in relation to the content of his teaching, his mystical theology; and secondly in relation to the expressions of his poetry, expressions of course which reveal his mysticism. Here I use the necessary distinction between *mystical theology*, the teaching substance; and *mysticism*, the experiential activity of that doctrine.

John's mystical theology

Firstly, then, the content of his teaching. This in John reaches the climax and the apex of all Christian mystical tradition. Notice that I use the words *climax* and *apex*: because it is not that what John teaches is radically new or totally different from what the Masters and Mistresses taught before him. He stands fully in the mainstream of Christian mystical tradition. The same questions have been asked and are still legitimately asked about John as have been asked about his predecessors: for whom is he writing? Is it all the baptised or merely those who have already taken the evangelical counsels and are seeking perfection?

Can the exact background of influence to his mystical doctrine be determined? In John's case is it Meister Eckhart, *Devotio Moderna* or is it a fusion of Muslim and Arabic and Southern Spanish elements? Is the main influence upon him ultimately the neo-Platonism of Dionysius the Areopagite?[8]

Moreover, much of what John says or teaches, much of the vocabulary used, is a different way of saying the same thing as his predecessors. How then does John absorb, excel and surpass all before and, for that matter, all since? Is it in the content of his teaching, his mystical theology?

There are two prongs to this answer: firstly he excels in the clarity, logic, precision and detail of his analysis of the mystical life and its demands and of what is involved at every stage of the journey to perfection: and this, in spite of his not finishing, or the loss of the end of, the commentary on *The Dark Night*.

Secondly, and deeply related to this logic, what is unique is the level of his insistence on the principle of total detachment from everything, not only at the final stages of the mystical journey of the union of the soul with God but as a natural prerequisite for beginning that journey. I will examine the second point first:

Total detachment

John's doctrine of detachment will, I hope, become clearer and fit into perspective as we look at the logical sequences of his teaching. But, before we look at that logical development, it is essential to be clear about this fundamental principle of John's mystical theology: in order to begin the mystical journey of the soul's union with God it is necessary that the soul become detached from everything that is not God: the individual who wishes to grow towards spiritual perfection must strip himself of, and be stripped of, all that is normal and familiar. Nothing must come between the individual and God. And so John is known as the *Doctor de la Nada*, The Doctor of Nothingness. The advice in *The Ascent I, 13 (11)* reads like a litany:

> To reach satisfaction in all
>   desire its possession in nothing.
> To come to possess all
>   desire the possession of nothing.
> To arrive at being all
>   desire to be nothing.
> To come to the knowledge of all
>   desire the knowledge of nothing.

> To come to the pleasure you have not
> > you must go by a way in which you enjoy not.
> To come to the knowledge you have not
> > you must go by a way in which you know not.
> To come to the possession you have not
> > you must go by a way in which you possess not.
> To come to be what you are not
> > you must go by a way in which you are not.

Nothing: *Nada*. When he was at Los Martires he used to give the nuns a drawing of Mount Carmel based upon this passage from *The Ascent* — but it was a drawing composed totally of words and lines — not of plastic images — and at the centre are the words *nada, nada, nada, nada, nada, nada*. And at the top of the mountain of Carmel he wrote 'and even here, *nada*'. Nothing.

John certainly developed in his thoughts on this *nada* over a long period of time; but in the end, he came to insist on detachment in many areas that his predecessors and contemporaries regarded as perfectly legitimate, at least at the beginning of spiritual progress. He defines himself consciously, I believe, and certainly we can define him over and against the teaching of other mystics. Here I wish to take four examples to illustrate the all-embracing nature of John's demands:

1. Firstly, detachment with regard to images, statues, pictures or any representation of Christ. Teresa herself informs us that at first when he joined the Reform, he loved to draw and carve crosses out of wood. He himself drew the crucified after a vision he is reported to have had at the Convent of the Incarnation. But gradually his own need for such aids decreased to the point of teaching that they can be inherently dangerous and harmful for spiritual growth. If images are used, 'the faithful man' John says, 'must immediately raise his mind beyond the object to what is represented by the image' (*Ascent III, 37,2*). This was one area where John's orthodoxy was suspect, especially as this area of detachment, John insists, also includes detachment from devotion, special places of prayer, i.e. churches and festivals of the Church.

2. Secondly, the detachment John demands is not merely from visible images but even from mental imagination of the scene or person portrayed by the image, or even by the pages of the Scriptures.

   The imagining of Christ crucified, or at the column, or in some other scene [John says], or of God seated on a throne with resplendent majesty . . . the soul will have to empty itself of these images if it is to reach divine union. . .

In this John is far removed from St Ignatius, for example, with his insistence on mental meditation as in the *Spiritual Exercises*.

> Imagine Christ Our Lord before you hanging on the cross . . . and so seeing him in such a condition — meditate upon the thoughts which come into your imagination . . .[9]

And John is equally removed from the strong stream of mystical tradition expressed clearly, for example, by St Bernard, who encourages mental meditation upon the humanity of Christ at the initial stages of the spiritual journey.[10]

3. Thirdly, John demands detachment from all spiritual and visionary experiences and voices from God; and physical experiences such as a levitation which might develop from them. He does not deny the *existence* of such experiences — he himself is reported to have levitated many times — but *never* mentions such personal experiences. Nor does he accept that such experiences might be part of, or show any development in the spiritual life.

   > One must never rely on them or accept them (he teaches). A man should rather flee from them completely, and have no desire to determine whether they be good or bad. (*Ascent II, 11,2*)

4. Fourthly, John demands detachment not from the use of symbols and images or illustrations as such in his doctrine, but from their use as expressing or explaining the logical development of his teaching.

All John's treatises are attempts not to enflesh with symbol but to denude and de-symbolise. The gorgeous landscapes with their flora and fauna, images such as ladders, honey, birdlime, rays of the sun showing up dust, all such images which he uses are not part of the content of his teaching, but prior to it. In other words, the imagery of creation is preliminary to and not part of John's mystical doctrine. The Bride of the Canticle looks at the world with all its images and sees it as speaking of God's absence. Compare this with Francis of Assisi's Canticle of Cosmic Praise. The only symbol John allows as part of his mystical theology is, of course, the anti-symbol of the Night.

Detachment from real images and from mental imagination, from spiritual experiences and from symbols and images to describe the logical development of his teaching: compare all these with Teresa — her holy picture of the Saviour; her experiences such as being talked to by Christ, or her transverberation in which she delights so much, let alone her levitations; her developing images of buckets and wells, of drops of water, rain, the ocean. Although John and Teresa are in fundamental agreement about the end of the process, the union of the soul with God, one can argue very cogently that John goes out of his way to contradict Teresa's presentation of that process; and almost to despise her continued autobiographical reference to her experiences of the process. John the theologian, as opposed to John the poet, did not write an autobiography and never makes any autobiographical references.

We must draw nearer to the heart of John's insistence on detachment and of his mistrust of experiences, images, symbols and creation. Because he is not merely issuing a warning against the spiritual excesses and superstition of his own generation, and there were enough of these, but he is carrying to its logical conclusion his scholastic theology. Like all scholastics, he accepts as a natural corollary that a person in some way becomes what he or she loves (*Ascent I, 4*); so that if desire and knowledge are turned to the imperfection of creation, that means one cannot know and love God the Creator. But more fully than his predecessors and contemporaries, John takes this to its inexorable conclusion: 'in its growth, the soul must be stripped of all things created, and of its own actions and abilities' (*Ascent II, 4*).

This all-embracing element of detachment in John's doctrine is called 'the principle of essential likeness' by Pope John Paul II, who wrote his doctoral dissertation on *Doctrina de fide apud Sanctum Joannem a Cruce*, defended on 19 June 1948 at the Angelicum, and now happily translated into English. The Pope sees this principle as being of fundamental importance and concludes as follows:

> The entire teaching of the Mystical Doctor on faith is developed in an organic way and according to a strictly logical deduction from the one principle that is also the principle underlying all his mystical doctrine. The principle, stated in chapter 8 of Book 2 of the *Ascent*, can be designated as the principle of essential likeness. The Mystical Doctor states that there is no essential likeness between God and any creature, for the divine essence infinitely transcends the essence of any creature, however perfect.[11]

Analysis of the soul's progress

Such teaching on detachment enhances and even causes the clarity, logic, precision and detail of John's analysis of the soul's progress. This analysis is a masterpiece of psychological insight.

To this, the second half of our enquiry into the content of John's teaching, we must turn.

It is, of course, John's description of the soul's journey to perfection, where he states as exhaustively as possible the human pre-condition for making God's grace fully one's own, where he uses and builds upon his characteristic vocabulary of the *Night*, which surpasses in its depths the nakedness of the author of the *Cloud of Unknowing* and of all the mystics before him. John tells us at the very beginning of *The Ascent* why the journey must be called Night:

> We can offer three reasons for calling this journey towards union with God a night.
>
> The first has to do with the point of departure, because the individual must deprive himself of his appetite for worldly possessions. This denial and privation is like a night for all his senses.
>
> The second reason refers to the means or road along which a person travels to this union. Now this road is faith, and for the intellect faith is also like a dark night.
>
> The third pertains to the point of arrival, namely God. God is also a dark night to man in his life. These three nights pass through a soul, or better, the soul passes through them in order to reach divine union with God.

Having discussed his reason for the use of the term 'night' John explains that there are two nights: the Night of the Senses; and the Night of the Spirit. Each of these nights has an active and a passive phase. In each case, it is easier to understand the active night as a deliberate activity engaged in by the individual to clear the path for God's activity; and the passive night as the actual experience of God's activity in the life of the individual; as John puts it, God's 'communication to the soul'.

John's Night of the Senses is more or less about physical concerns, the Night of the Spirit about non-physical concerns. While there is a natural element of chronology — of moving from one stage to another in the journey to perfection — it is important to realise that John's nights are not merely chronological, with one development following after the other, as a cursory reading of his works might imply. John's image of the human person is fundamentally that of psychosomatic unity. The physical night does not merely precede the spiritual one and then disappear, but continues alongside it. Similarly the active part of the night does not merely precede the passive, but the two can mingle together. All the elements he describes, as he says, are part of one and the same night, which has to become darker before the dawn.

However, we must press on to following John's analytical development of the Night.

The active Night of the Senses consists of training the body to withstand all physical desire and preference. John calls this night 'the mortification of the appetites and the denial of pleasure in all things'. This 'all things' includes, among others, possessions, food, health, security, and the desire for wisdom and knowledge. Here is the proper place for John's famous counsels (*The Ascent* I, 13, 6):

> Endeavour to be inclined always:
> not to the easiest, but to the most difficult;
> not to the most delightful, but to the harshest;
> not to the most gratifying, but to the less pleasant;
> not to what means rest to you, but to hard work;
> not to the consoling, but to the unconsoling;
> not to the most, but to the least;
> not to the most highest and most precious, but to the
>   lowest and most despised;
> not to wanting something, but to wanting nothing;
> do not go about looking for the best of temporal things,
> but for the worst, and desire to enter into complete
> nudity, emptiness, and poverty in everything
>   in the world.

Only by following this advice can we be sure that we have started on the road to perfection. The passive Night of the Senses is the actual experience of the sense of deprivation and abandonment of all that is secure and of all that is familiar, a sense of being lost.

The Night of the Spirit, the Dark Night, strikes at the very roots of illusion and systematically reduces human spiritual activity, as opposed to physical activity, to one act of faith and longing.

The Ascent describes the active Night of the Spirit, the human side of the process — as with the activity of the Night of the Senses. There is described what we can do to identify and interpret the conditions; the habits of mind we must cultivate and the dangers we must avoid. This active Night of the Spirit is the purgation of the self, divided scholastically into memory, intellect and will. During the activity of this night the intellect must be reduced to faith; memory to hope; and will to love.

Briefly, I wish to explain what John teaches about the first of these — the reduction of the intellect to faith (*Ascent II*). In concentrating on this area we not only see John at his most distinctive but we will also be given a further key to understand Karol Wojtyla's doctoral thesis, which centres on this subject.

To explain his teaching, John makes a division of the types of knowledge that the intellect can receive; one natural, the other supernatural. The natural means all the knowledge for which the human intellect suffices by its very nature, receiving it directly through the senses or by its own power. For this type of knowledge, objects will have to be present either in themselves or in their likeness (*Ascent II, 3, 2*). Supernatural knowledge signifies that which exceeds the natural power of the intellect — knowledge that the intellect could never attain by its own efforts, because the knowledge was not gained through sense, or experience of the things themselves or their representations. John gave this as an example:

> If a man were informed that on a certain island there was an animal whose like or kind he had never seen, he would then have no more idea or image of that animal in his mind than previously. . . (*Ascent II, 3, 2*).

The knowledge that a man would have to have in order to imagine that animal must come from a source other than natural knowledge; that source is supernatural knowledge. John further divides supernatural knowledge into corporeal and spiritual. Corporeal supernatural knowledge is imagination and fantasy. Spiritual knowledge is divided into distinct and particular knowledge on the one hand, and on the other that which is confused, general and dark. The distinct particular knowledge is of four kinds: visions, revelations, locutions and spiritual feelings. The general and dark knowledge is of one kind only, contemplation given in faith. After explaining all the types of supernatural knowledge, John proceeds to reject all of them as a means of spiritual progress. In a devastating catalogue, unparalleled before or since, he exhibits a profound sensitivity of the risks of self-deception in the spiritual life. Remember what we saw when examining John's doctrine of detachment: nothing is acceptable as a means of progress. The Pope concludes thus:

> This dark active night of the spirit is a privation of the desire for anything that is not God; it is related to love because this night prevents one loving any created or natural form; it is related to faith, because faith unites the soul to divinity — but does not transform the soul intrinsically as in the case of the beatific vision. Thus, because of the mystic of light and darkness, faith is properly described as a dark night or non-vision, and is at the same time the cause of the dark night that characterises the entire passage to union.[12]

What John says about the purification of the memory and will (*Ascent III*) repeats much of what he says about the active purification of the intellect. The processes connected with the memory involve the stripping away of the securities possessed by the mind, in so far as it is shaped by forms received from creatures. The will is purged by a growing detachment from the four passions of joy, hope, fear and grief. He in fact never completes this catalogue, but he does give a very full description of the purgation of the passion of joy, and what he means by joy does cover any experience of gratification of the spirit. He naturally teaches that moral uprightness must be sought and prized, but one must be completely detached from rejoicing over supposed moral perfection; only then are the 'passions' reduced to love of God.

John's teaching on the passive Night of the Spirit is found in *The Dark Night of the Soul*; as with the passive Night of the Senses, the passive Night of the Spirit is the actual experiential level of God's purifying activity. It is not just a sequence of decisions to do without spiritual consolation; it is the actual lived and felt absence of consolation, the sense of God as distant, rejecting and hostile. It is the experience of the movement away from order, form, structure and reality, producing a shapelessness which is both frustrating and alarming. John indicates that this must inevitably involve an acute sense of rejection, humiliation and worthlessness, in short a dissolution of the sense of self. This and only this is the necessary prelude to union with God.

The journey, with all its devastation, is now over. The movement towards nothing does not bring annihilation, but total fulfilment. John explicitly recognises that the journey is dangerous psychologically, though of course without using the latter word. Do not attempt it alone, he says again and again. You must have a spiritual director who knows what he is doing and how much you can take. 'The virtuous soul that is alone and without a master is like a lone burning coal; it will grow colder rather than hotter.' (*Sayings of light and love*)[13]

What is this union with God at the end of the journey? True to his principle of detachment John does not tell us what it is from a subjective point of view. He does not tell us when it happened in his own life. When asked, he wrote the poem *The Living Flame of Love*. From that and from the latter part of *The Spiritual Canticle* we can see that he implies the state of union to be a sense of God constantly living in the soul, of God's goodness in all things, of the warmth of reciprocal love. The union with God involves, as many commentators have mentioned, a re-conversion to creatures and to creation; to know God's creatures and God's creation in a contemplative fashion. In his *Prayer of an Enamoured Soul,* he declares:

> Mine are the Heavens and mine is the earth;
>> mine are the people, —
> the righteous are mine and mine are the sinners;
>> the Angels are mine . . . and the mother of God,
>> and all things are mine; —
> and God Himself is mine and for me, —
>> for Christ is mine and all for me.
> What then dost thou ask for and seek, my soul?
>> Thine is all this, and it is all for thee.

This is only possible after the detachments of the Nights, precise recognition of the stages involved and the following through of their logical progressions.

Mysticism of the poetry

Having briefly outlined the content of John's mystical theology and the reasons for its importance, we must now turn to the second reason why John is pre-eminent: his mysticism, as expressed in his poetry. The rich images of his poetry are, as I have already pointed out, preliminary to and not part of his mystical teaching; but without doubt his poems themselves are not only part of, but coincide with, his own mystical experience.

The highest compliment to John's poetry was paid when John was made patron of Spanish poets by the Spanish Government in 1952: this itself is a testimony to the place his poetry holds in Spanish literature, despite the fact that John wrote only three major poems (*The Dark Night, The Spiritual Canticle* and *The Living Flame of Love*); ten smaller poems and ten romances (the authenticity of which has been doubted). He seems to have had a natural talent and certainly a natural inclination to write poetry. On making his first profession at the Calced Priory, we are told that he wrote some verses 'in heroic verse and pastoral style', which are unfortunately lost. On joining the Reform, he eschewed poetry, but the depression of prison in Toledo in 1578 seems to have revived his poetic enthusiasm. Much has been written about John's poetry, but probably the most authoritative study is in Spanish by Damaso Alonso in his work *La Poesia de San Juan de la Cruz*[14] fortunately distilled for the non-Spanish reader in Brenan's work. Alonso divides the literary influences on John into Spanish and biblical. The Spanish ones are fascinating, but we can only glance at them *en passant*. They appear to have been above all popular songs, the type that would have been sung in the streets, and a poet called Garcilaso de la Vega, a courtier under the Emperor Charles V. Alonso sees the very existence of John's three major poems, along with their metre and subject matter, as stemming from the influence of this poet de la Vega. For it was this latter poet who introduced the Italian renaissance style to Spain, the hendecasyllable, the refinement of Castilian idiom, and the drawing on Renaissance poetic themes including a refined sense of beauty, artificial pastoral scenes and a certain sensuality. All these attributes are found in John's three major poems.

But however important the Spanish literary background for the metre of his poetry, it was not, I believe, so all-embracing as the influences of the Scriptures for the inspiration, to a certain extent the form, and certainly the content of John's poetry. While it is true that all the great saints knew their Scriptures and used them, John not only parallels but excels others in his assimilation of them. Cardinal Wiseman put it neatly in 1864:

> The source of John's most numerous and happiest elucidations are to be found in the inspired Word of God . . . it is an impartial familiarity . . . every book of scripture is equally ready to hand, to prove more formally, occasionally to illustrate, every one of his propositions. For the first purpose he must have deeply studied the Sacred text; for the second its expressions must have been his very household words.[15]

John, in fact, uses 597 quotations from the Old Testament and 327 from the New Testament. But of course the influence of the Scriptures is much greater than that of direct quotation. In his prose commentary on *The Ascent* John says he uses the Scriptures for everything — *para todo*. Fr Fabrizio Forresti[16] has argued cogently that John's double Night of the Senses and of the Spirit have at their methodological base the theological principle of transcendence as expressed in the first and second commandment: the unity of God and the principle of total love as the first, and the incomparability of God as the second. From this perspective, the centre of John's poetry and teaching is nothing other than the centre of the Divine Revelation made on Mount Sinai.

While much can be said in favour of Fr Forresti, his hypothesis of the methodological use of the Commandments can never be proven, as John does not give the first and second Commandments, as such, an all-embracing role. However the influence of the *Song of Songs*, as a methodological base, at least for his poems *The Canticle* and *The Dark Night* requires no proof. Like many saints before him, these Hebrew poems of the *Song of Songs* provided rich inspiration for John; but for him they were also the constitutive base of these two poems, as any reading of them shows.

John might have drawn inspiration from the many commentaries and writings by his predecessors on the allegorical interpretations of the *Song of Songs*, for example those of Augustine, Bernard and Peter Damian. The richness and the beauty of the text could have been mediated to him: but, in the end, the tempo, the exhilaration, the speed of movement, the landscapes, mountains, rivers, valleys, dawns, breezes, rocky caves, mountain thickets, lions, antelope, birds and flowers, and indeed, whole phrases, show John's direct and commanding use of the Scriptures. This also, of course, highlights his command of Spanish and Latin. Since he did not know Hebrew or Greek and since at the time of his composition there was no official Spanish version of the *Song of Songs*, he was dependent solely on the Vulgate.

Although we have, albeit briefly, examined John's poetry last, his poems are, of course, prior to his prose; his mysticism is prior to his mystical theology; John the poet is prior to John the theologian. But does either help the average Christian of today? Remembering Allison Peers' point that John is not comprehensible solely but only primarily to contemplatives, and that anyone who really wants to learn from John can do so, I think we can answer the above question in the affirmative.[17]

We can learn from John the poet; firstly, apart from inspiring us to learn Spanish in order to grasp the beauty of the original, John's poems nudge us, push us, and continually place us in the presence of the source of all Christian mysticism, the inspired Word of God. The poems, full of the vivid reality of the Scriptures, are a constant reminder that there can be no truly Christian mysticism, or even an understanding of Christian mysticism, without the use and assimilation of the Scriptures, so that they become a lived-out, expressive reality in the life of the individual.

Secondly, we can learn from John the theologian, the teacher. Very important in this area are his deep psychological insights. Here I would reiterate his insistence on a fully informed spiritual director, and his awareness, an awareness that we particularly need to have, of the devastating dangers of self-deception in all areas of our lives. More specifically, John's analysis of the process leading to union and peace through the Nights has been accepted and developed by some psychotherapists. Thomas Tyrrell for example, (of the House of Affirmation, in Whitinsville, Massachusetts) in his book *Urgent Longings*, itself a phrase from the poem *The Dark Night*, uses John's logical analysis and terminology of the Nights to reflect upon the experiences of infatuation, human intimacy and contemplative love. Tyrrell insists on a positive acceptance of the experience of infatuation — urgent longings — as being a painful but necessary part of growth experience leading to personal integration.[18] The enthusiasm of love he describes as infatuation's Active Night; and the experience following of shame, guilt and isolation, he describes as love's Passive Night. The unitive stage of psychological integration, love's peace and stillness, occurs only after the loneliness and the searching, the urgency and illusion, the enthusiasm and the disappointment of love's disturbing darkness.

If we move away from clinical psychology as such we find that John further helps the average Christian in the two areas of challenge and encouragement; that is true, of course, for all the saints, but John's challenge and encouragement become distinctive in the light of his whole teaching. The challenge is never to be content with anything less than perfection, a challenge that of necessity brings with it a constant desire to improve. The encouragement is not to despair while we are trying. A sense of frustration and futility, of wondering what the whole of life is about, of even doubting the existence of God — experiences so common among us all — not only could be, but are, part of the Dark Night. Where most of us differ from John, of course, is that we remain in the Dark Night during this life, and the state of union does not come until after our death.

7

St Francis de Sales

by
Kevin McDonald

The purpose of this essay is to present a portrait of St Francis de Sales. To create that portrait, I will trace the saint's life in its general outline, and dwell on certain events and moments in that life which can best illustrate the kind of person he was, the things that influenced him most, and his significance for Christians today.

Schools and education

He was born in 1567 in Thorens, near Annecy, which today is in France but which was then part of the Duchy of Savoy. Savoy comprised parts of what are, today, France, Switzerland and Italy: it is a mountainous stretch of country and Francis de Sales belonged to one of its ancient noble families. Throughout his life, he was to remain deeply attached to the country of his birth. He was to resist offers of ecclesiastical preferment in France and instead gave his life to ministering within his homeland.

Francis was the eldest of thirteen children; his first school was the Capuchin College in Annecy. At the age of fifteen, he went to the Jesuit College de Clermont in Paris. He travelled there with a servant and with a priest who stayed with him as his private tutor. The College de Clermont was noted for its moral discipline at a time of general moral disorder. It was also a school which provided thorough education in the humanities, and here, I suggest, we have an important key to Francis de Sales. At school he learnt Latin, Greek philosophy, as well as acquiring all the other accomplishments that would be expected of a man of his class, such as fencing and dancing.

He imbibed the spirit of the Renaissance, that rediscovery of classical art and literature which was the most important cultural movement in Europe between the fourteenth and sixteenth centuries. The Renaissance was the rediscovery of the beauty of ancient Greece and Rome, and was inevitably also a rebirth of humanism. The Renaissance was a complex movement whose effects on religion and philosophy were complex too. For some the new humanism brought suspicion of many aspects of Catholicism, especially the taking of religious vows and the entry into religious orders, since these seemed to constitute a denial of the truly human.

But for others, the new learning brought with it insights into the spiritual nature of man. For those who espoused the spirit of the Renaissance the scholastic philosophy of the Middle Ages seemed knotty and tortuous. They reacted against it. Francis de Sales was supremely a humanist: his philosophy was eminently simple and straightforward. He was not interested in theories and arguments for their own sake: his interest was essentially in man.

During his education in Paris, Francis was welcomed into the homes of members of the Paris nobility who knew his family. He seems to have been a warm and friendly person but clearly showed a certain reserve in personal relationships. He had always been devout, and towards the end of his time in Paris he experienced what was to be the only major spiritual crisis of his life. He developed a terrible sense that he was destined to be eternally separated from God. It was a traumatic time for him, but it was something he overcame as he gradually recovered his sense of the reality of God and of God's mercy and goodness. It is significant for his personal development that it was the positive perception of the truth of God that dispelled the darkness of his time of crisis. Having come through the experience he returned to Savoy for the first time in six years in 1588. He had a brief holiday at home but was soon away again to complete his education.

University and theology

Francis now travelled south, to the University of Padua, where he took a doctorate in law and thus fulfilled his father's plans for him. But he read for a doctorate in theology at the same time. This was his own idea and was obviously bound up with his growing sense that he was called to be a priest. So his theological formation took place in Padua and we may pause to consider some of the characteristics of his unique theological vision that was taking shape during these years.

His theological ideas are of a piece with his general humanist perspective. It has been remarked that a true humanist will always experience, at one stage or another, a conflict between the claims of the spiritual life and the claims of human fulfilment. In the person of Francis de Sales and in his theology that conflict was remarkably and conspicuously resolved. It was resolved without any dualism because Francis experienced within himself that man has a natural tendency towards God, and this discovery became a part of his whole outlook.

Since men and women are part of God's plan, it is natural for them to love their creator. God is the source of goodness and beauty: all goodness and beauty disclose God to us and awaken a sensitivity to the attractiveness of God. Our understanding never experiences such profound joy as when we think about God. This theological vision represents an integration of human and spiritual values, a fusion of devotion and humanity. It is precisely here that I find his significance for contemporary life and contemporary theology.

In our culture no one particularly expects that a person with a great love for the arts and the humanities will be religious. In fact, when we discover that a famous poet, philosopher or musician is a committed Christian, we are likely to be surprised. It is common, too, for people who hold human values very dear to regard Christianity as something that limits people, something that restricts their freedom of development and of expression. Michael Muller[1] in his book on Francis diagnoses this situation with a very telling phrase: he says that in the modern world we have witnessed the 'secularisation of joy'. Joy is sought and thought to be possible independently of God. Francis, who was fully sensitive to all the joy of life, saw that God is the source and ground of human joy and in making this affirmation he was able to present a genuinely unified view of man. The gratitude and joy engendered in the human spirit by belief in God is the source of optimism and confidence of a kind that could form the basis of a Christian civilisation in which the individual person can find himself and be himself. Throughout Francis' writings there is a continual insistence on the importance for the Christian soul of fostering and preserving a happy and joyful temperament.

What is Francis de Sales' significance for contemporary theology? It is impossible here to answer that question fully but I will give one pointer to his contemporary relevance as I see it. One of the most important theological writers today is Hans Urs von Balthasar. His major work, *The Glory of the Lord*,[2] is a theological aesthetic. What this means is that he takes the logic of beauty as his key to understanding the Christian mystery. For von Balthasar, man's relationship to God is appropriately understood in terms of the model of man's contemplation of beauty. This perspective differs significantly from those ways of understanding Christianity that see it in terms of human self-realisation. By presenting Christian faith in terms of the model of aesthetic contemplation, von Balthasar is able to maintain the total givenness of God's revelation in Christ. In the introduction, the author makes a critical survey of those writers, both Catholic and Protestant, who have contributed to theological aesthetics.[3] One of the authors mentioned is René de Chateaubriand who in 1802 wrote a work entitled *Le Génie du Christianisme*. Chateaubriand lists those people who anticipated him in his theological approach, and they include Origen, Augustine, Francis de Sales and Pascal. There is a tradition to which Francis belongs; he shared a particular outlook with others who preceded and followed him. He was one of those who have been attracted by the beauty of the Christian revelation and have responded to the mystery with enthusiasm and devotion. His writings today are able to draw others into the mystery by stimulating their desire to grow into the beauty and holiness of God.

Ordination and the Chablais

Francis spent three years in Padua gaining doctorates in both law and theology. He returned home and then had the task of getting his father to accept the fact that he was going to be a priest. His father wanted him to have a political and diplomatic career, but was persuaded to consent to Francis becoming a priest, partly through the good offices of a relation of theirs who managed to secure for the young man a very senior position in the diocese, that of Provost of the Chapter. Francis did not really want this kind of rapid preferment, though it would not have been unusual for someone of his class, but he accepted it and was ordained priest at Annecy on 21 December 1593. What followed would have been a difficult and challenging task for any young priest and it was to occupy him for the next four years.

To open up this phase in the saint's life, we have to introduce into this study another historical movement, one that had already changed the face of Europe, namely the Reformation. The diocese into which Francis was ordained was the diocese of Geneva. This city had become a centre of Protestant Christianity. Geneva itself and the surrounding district had become almost completely Protestant, and the Protestants wielded political as well as spiritual power throughout the whole area. This of course meant that the Catholic Bishop of Geneva could not reside there; in fact he lived at Annecy. Catholics who went to Geneva at all did so at great personal risk.

In 1593 a region near Lake Geneva known as the Chablais was returned by the City of Geneva to the Duchy of Savoy. After sixty years in Protestant hands it was being returned to a Catholic ruler and Francis was given the task of trying to reconvert the people of the Chablais to the Catholic faith. During these years in a very hostile environment he was protected, because he needed to be, by the Duke of Savoy's soldiers and he achieved a remarkable degree of success in his mission. The significance of this experience was that it brought him out of an academic atmosphere and into contact with some of the very brutal facts about human nature and the realities of life. Also, at this stage some aspects of his character gain sharper focus. In his dealings with the Protestants he was remarkably courteous by the standards of the day. Courtesy and gentleness became two of the most character-istic features of his personality. He was also unswervingly firm and loyal to the Catholic Church and, in particular, to the decrees of the Council of Trent.

Coadjutor and bishop

When he was recalled from the Chablais, it was to become coadjutor to the Bishop of Geneva; that meant that he would eventually succeed the Bishop and so he now became much more involved in high-level political and ecclesiastical life although he was not immediately consecrated a bishop. He was sent to Rome to represent the Bishop at the *ad limina* meeting with the Pope, and in 1601 he was sent on a diplomatic mission to the King of France, Henri IV. The king was very much a man of this world and he made a shrewd summing-up of Francis de Sales after his meeting with him:

> A rare bird, this Monsieur de Genève: he is devout and also learned; and not only devout and learned, but at the same time a gentleman. A very rare combination.[4]

This last remark, 'also a gentleman', gives a shade more light on Francis. When we talk about someone being a gentleman we are not usually talking about their faith or their virtue or their morals. We are more likely to be saying something about their manners and their general bearing. Francis de Sales was an essentially holy person who also had the grace and courtesy which are part of what we normally mean when we call someone a gentleman. This was of immediate importance in Paris at that time since there were people in and around the court who, amid appalling moral decadence, were struggling to live a deep Christian life. These people spotted Francis as someone who spoke their language, who was one of them and who would be able to lead them to God. Foremost among these was the famous Madame Acarie who was the first of the many people to whom he became spiritual director.

His mission in Paris completed, he returned home, and it was while he was on his journey back to Savoy that the Bishop of Geneva died. Francis made a retreat and on 8 December 1602, at the age of thirty-five, he was consecrated bishop of Geneva. He was to remain bishop of his home diocese for the rest of his life, refusing, as I have said, high ecclesiastical appointments in France. The picture of his subsequent life that has come down to us is one of enormous industry; preaching, writing, giving missions, going on visitations, as well as dealing with constant administrative and political business. But most remarkable of all was his relationship of spiritual director to a wide range of different sorts of people; among these, one relationship grew up which was and is outstanding.

Madame de Chantal

In 1604, the Bishop of Geneva was invited to preach a series of Lenten sermons in Dijon. Also in Dijon at the time was the young archbishop-elect of Bourges and with him was his sister who had come to Dijon especially to hear the Lenten sermons. We know her today as St Jane Frances de Chantal. At that time she was Madame Jeanne Françoise Frémyot de Chantal, a young woman with four small children whose husband had quite recently been killed in a hunting accident. Still reeling under the shock of her husband's death, she was a devout and determined woman who was also living in very difficult circumstances. She and her children were staying with her father-in-law in what was a very trying situation indeed. She had also acquired a spiritual director who was clearly out of his depth. From this meeting with the Bishop of Geneva grew a very deep friendship, a correspondence (letters which are spiritual classics) and eventually a new religious community: the Visitation Order.

The correspondence between them began when Francis returned to Annecy after preaching the sermons in Dijon. Today we have nearly all Francis' letters to Jane Frances de Chantal but none of her letters to him. Francis kept and annotated all her letters and on his death the letters were returned to her by Francis' brother. She destroyed them all, and it is impossible to know exactly why. We learn a good deal about her from Francis' letters and what stands out on every page is his great love and affection for her. In a letter shortly after the Dijon meeting, he says:

> The more I feel distanced from you exteriorly, the more I feel joined and tied to you interiorly. May God perfect in you his work which is your desire and design to come to Christian perfection.[5]

That letter is dated 3 May 1604. In a letter of 14 October of the same year, after becoming her spiritual director, he gives a long and very detailed reply to her questions about prayer and about temptations, and he adds:

> Every affection differs in some particular way from every other. My affection for you has a special quality which consoles me infinitely and, if all were said, is of great profit to me. Take this as a matter of fact and have no doubt about it. I did not want to speak as openly as this, but one word leads to another; besides, I feel you will know how to take it.[6]

I draw attention to these expressions of affection because it is important both to give them their full value and to see them in their context. Francis de Sales was a very warm person but he was also a person of quite unusual spiritual seriousness. Francis' love for Madame de Chantal was inextricably bound up with his concern for her soul; everything he writes to her is written with a view to her spiritual growth. A study of their relationship gives us a picture of civilised humanity as it opens itself to the transforming power of grace.

This is not the place to catalogue all the advice he gave to her in his letters; sufficient to say that she suffered very distressing temptations against faith and great affliction of spirit, and his words to her, as to all his correspondents, are highly personal, directed to her specific needs, and always patient and painstaking.

The introduction to the devout life

Madame de Chantal was only one of the people he guided. Important in a different kind of way was Madame de Charmoisy, wife of an ambassador of the Duke of Savoy. She put herself under his direction in 1607 and Francis gave her a series of spiritual instructions that he had begun to compile the year he was made bishop. She showed these instructions to a Jesuit priest who on reading them strongly urged Francis to have them published. This he did, and in 1609 there appeared the first edition of one of the great classics of western spirituality, the *Introduction to the Devout Life*. In this book, his wisdom becomes available to the Church as a whole. If we now consider some of its themes, we can see how his character and his theological vision created a particular style of spirituality.

The novelty of the book is that it was not composed for people in enclosed religious life; it was written for people who live in the secular world but who wish to pursue the 'devout' life. In the first section it becomes clear that what Francis means by the 'devout' life is a life of charity, a life of love of God. But there is a particular nuance here, because the 'devout' life, *la vie dévote*, involves and suggests enthusiasm for the spiritual journey. He says that we must not only have charity; we must practice it cheerfully and with zest. Francis observes that most people actually regard the devout life as a misery, as a sort of 'none life', but they fail to realise that interior devotion of the heart is a real and complete joy for those who undertake it. The maintenance of spiritual joy is something crucial. It is clearly from his experience as a spiritual director that he points out that sadness disturbs the soul: it leads to disquiet and inordinate fear: it breeds distaste for prayer and can leave the soul almost paralysed. It is important to preserve equanimity amid change and we will do that, provided we keep our will fixed on God. An inviolable resolution to tend always towards God will preserve equanimity of spirit. True devotion is a matter of seeking and doing the will of God.

St Francis says that devotion is for everyone, no matter what their state in life. But we must never undertake a form of devotion that is incompatible with our calling or status. The devout life is to be lived in the context of each individual's particular calling or vocation. But that does not mean that people should try to pursue it unaided, and on their own. Implore God, the writer says, to send you someone after his own heart, someone who understands your soul. When you have found him, trust him and bless God. He will put into your heart whatever is necessary for your happiness. What is involved from then on is the purification of the soul and for this to happen, what is needed first and foremost is patience.

This theme, in particular, is one that is echoed frequently in his letters: to live the devout life people have to be patient with all those things that afflict them and are unavoidably part of their lives. Be patient, he says, with serious things but also with the many annoyances and inconveniences that make up life. Be patient with whatever God wills, as he wills it and when he wills it. Especially, being patient means remaining calm and peaceful: we deal much more effectively with our problem if we react without any over-eagerness or passion. The secret of the devout life is to be free of those things and, instead, to rely on God's providence.

The first stage in the devout life must be purification from mortal sin. It is very useful, St Francis says, soon after embracing the devout life to make a General Confession of all the sins of one's life. But we must free our hearts not only from mortal sin but from attachment to it. Using one of his many images, he remarks that some people abstain from sin as a sick man abstains from melon — with great reluctance! So, free your hearts and you will experience the vitality that is the basis for the devout life.

A section of the treatise is devoted to prayer and the Sacraments. Prayer, the author says, opens the mind to the brightness of divine light, and the will to the warmth of heavenly love. When you pray, conform your heart to the sentiments you express. Better to say a short prayer, attending to the meaning of the words, than to say a lot of prayers without attention. If you are drawn into interior mental prayer, don't resist. St Francis gives a series of meditations which give practical help in organising one's prayer time. Prayer should begin with an acknowledgment of the presence of God; we should make resolutions on the basis of what is given to us in prayer time. In the morning, anticipate the opportunities and temptations that lie ahead, and at night make an examination of conscience. Stay recollected during the day; remember God; remember his presence. At least once a year the devout life must be re-established with resolutions about the renewal of one's whole life.

It is not surprising that Francis de Sales has things to say about the significance of friendship in the devout life. Friendship,the writer says, can be rooted and grounded in a variety of things. But if the things that ground a friendship are false or superficial, then so will the friendship be. Friendships based on sexual attraction that arise in a context that cannot lead to marriage, in fact lead to lust and dissipate the heart, they are a waste of time and are enervating because they give rise to unreal hopes and anticipations. They dissipate moral and spiritual energy, stifle joy and disable us from really loving God:

> God asks all our love for having created, preserved and redeemed us. All the life within us is eaten up if we give ourselves to false friendship.[7]

Both in this work, and in a letter to Jane Frances in 1604, it is clearly his conviction that those who live the devout life can love one another on earth exactly as they will love one another in heaven. Relationships of this kind are really the only ones worth having. They can arise within marriage or outside marriage: the distinguishing feature is that true friendships are grounded in a shared pursuit of the devout life. And this is especially important, in the saint's view, for those who do not live in religious communities: those who travel across rough and tricky ground need to cling to one another. People in the secular world who seek devotion have different aims and objectives from those around them and need the support of spiritual friendship.

On the particular question of marriage, Francis says:

> God. . . with his invisible hand has fashioned the sacred bond of your marriage and given you to each other.[8]

Christ unites husband and wife with his blood in a union that is more difficult to break than the union of body and soul. But for love between husband and wife to prosper, it must be based on devotion: then they will sanctify one another.

So, the *Introduction to the Devout Life* is a clear, practical manual for those who wish to take their Christian life seriously. It became a classic in Francis' own lifetime; it was translated into various languages and went into numerous editions. It has stood the test of time. As I see it, the usefulness of the book lies simply in the fact that it starts where people are and it points a clear way forward.

Conclusion

One date in the life of St Francis de Sales that was important for future generations was 6 June 1610. It was then that he founded the first Visitation convent in Annecy. The initial community comprised Jane Frances and three companions. Jane Frances had been wanting to enter religious life for some time, but obviously could not do this while her children were still young. In fact she has often been criticised for leaving them when she did. Francis' idea in founding the new congregation was to have a religious community that was not enclosed and did not take solemn vows. For the first five years of the Visitation Order, that was how it was. In fact, they left the convent very little, but even that was considered too much by the Archbishop of Lyons, and when a Visitation convent was founded in his city, he expressed his disapproval of nuns being seen in the streets. Francis acquiesced with the Archbishop's view, and the Visitation became, and remained, an enclosed order. But his idea of an apostolic order of nuns was eventually realised by another of his friends, St Vincent de Paul. After Francis' death, Vincent de Paul undertook the spiritual direction of the Visitation Order and he also founded the Sisters of Charity, now the largest religious order in the Church.

It was for the Visitation nuns, now a purely contemplative order, that Francis wrote his other great work, the *Treatise on the Love of God*. This appeared in 1616 and is a full-scale exposition of his mystical theology. The fact that he was able to write this book is evidence of his continuing industry right up to the end of his life. He became increasingly involved in ecclesiastical and civil politics, in the work of the diocese, and in the growth of the Visitation Order.

He died on 28 December 1622, at the age of fifty-five, and was buried at the Visitation convent in Annecy. His friend and disciple, Jane Frances de Chantal, died twenty-four years later in 1646. He was canonised in 1655; she in 1767. The last word on St Francis de Sales may appropriately be given to that other friend and disciple, St Vincent de Paul, who sums up the genius of Francis de Sales as follows:

> Monseigneur de Sales had a burning desire to be the image of the Son of God. He conformed so well to this model, I know, that I have often asked myself with amazement how an ordinary human being, given the frailty of human nature, could reach so great a degree of perfection . . . going over his words in my mind, I felt such admiration that I would tend to see him as the man who reproduced most faithfully the Son of God living on earth.[9]

8

English recusant spirituality

by
Judith Champ

English recusant spirituality flowered for a little over 200 years, between the reign of Elizabeth and the end of the eighteenth century. It was the spirituality of a tiny minority of Christian England (at best only a few per cent of the population). That minority was persecuted more or less harshly throughout the period, by financial penalties, legal disabilities, social ostracism and, for the first half of the period, by torture, imprisonment and execution.

In many ways it was a closed community, anxious for its self-preservation, patiently and determinedly holding fast to faith. There was nothing (in the eyes of the world) to be gained from being a Catholic, and everything to be lost, but the community began to re-establish itself slowly as religious pluralism became possible. The renaissance of English Catholicism was based on the stalwart work of missionary clergy, trained abroad, on the loyalty of Catholic gentry and aristocracy whose material support was crucial, and on the devotion and persistence of a gradually increasing number of ordinary working men and women.

Recusant life was far from easy. Apart from the physical and economic threats and the social disadvantage which it brought, Catholicism was uncomfortable, often drab and routine. It required of most of its adherents, not the special courage of the martyr, but a sober persistence with scant support. Priests were few, chapels even fewer. Devotions were limited in scope and there was, by and large, a great need for Catholic self-motivation. The Catholic often had to be his own minister and spiritual director and the family was often his only community.

Tales of persecution and martyrdom led later generations to believe that Catholicism largely died out between the Elizabethan age and the nineteenth century and that devotional life was limited to secret Masses at dead of night. Historians have shown this to be untrue on both counts and the library of recusant devotional literature is immense, considering the size of the community and the circumstances in which it was produced. Until the late seventeenth century much of it was imported or printed secretly in England but in the eighteenth century Catholic printers and booksellers flourished openly in London.

The spirituality of the Catholic community is reflected in the most popular devotional works of the period. Two paradoxes present themselves in a consideration of Catholic recusant devotions: the first is that they are totally of their period, reflecting the rigour and sobriety of Catholic life mentioned above, yet some of them have retained a place in the canon of personal devotional reading up to and even beyond the Second Vatican Council. The second paradox is that although they are peculiarly and specifically English in their tone and content and were produced for a Catholic community whose way of life was in many ways remote from the Counter-Reformation, yet they are profoundly products of the European Counter-Reformation. It is these paradoxes which I propose to explore, concentrating particularly on the works of Richard Challoner but setting his work in the context of the recusant spiritual tradition.

Recusant devotional works in English began to appear during Elizabeth's reign, among the earliest being the translation of the revised Tridentine Roman Breviary, known as the *Primer*, and first translated in 1599.[1] This was obviously a Tridentine continuation of pre-Reformation devotions. In fact it had thirteenth century origins and provides the continuity in English devotional literature. Of the specifically post-Reformation products (i.e. those designed for the recusant community) the earliest and most popular was the *Manual*.[2] This was not the *Manual* for clergy, used in conducting the Sacraments, but a compilation of prayers, devotions and instructions (including some pre-Reformation material) translated and compiled in English.

The numerous editions of the *Manual* are really variations on a theme, with no authorised original version. It varied widely in size, number of prayers and the relative amount of instructions and devotion. It was thus adaptable and was in practice adapted to specific circumstances, thus reflecting the changing needs and different local circumstances of recusant life.

Characteristically, it consisted of a calendar, a section of religious instruction and doctrine, prayers and meditations for specific occasions, prayers and meditations for every day of the week, ending with a section of other prayers and litanies. The manual was not in any edition a straight translation, but borrowed from a diverse range of material, from Thomas More, the *Imitation*, the *Jesus Psalter* and from the pre-Reformation Primers of York and Sarum. Its structure rarely changed, though the actual content often did. That structure is important, since it became the structure of recusant daily devotional life. Virtually all editions until 1800 were governed to a greater or lesser degree by the division into the days of the week.

Traditionally the *Manual* was produced anonymously though a number of editions are identifiable. In the early seventeenth century it was edited and partly written by John Heigham (the first editions came from Rouen); later in the seventeenth century John Gother may have edited one *Manual*; from 1744 onwards Challoner certainly did. It reflected the hardships of recusancy in its production, originally in Rouen, in the early seventeenth century in secret in England, later possibly in Paris, and eventually in the eighteenth century openly in London.

However it also reflects a ready and persistent market for books of personal devotion; edition after edition of the *Manual* was produced until the nineteenth century. The *Manual* retained its popularity, but was quickly followed by other devotional works, including Edward Mayhew's *Paradise of Prayers and Meditations*, *The Key of Paradise*, John Austin's *Devotions in the Ancient Way of Offices*, and most significantly, Gother's *Instructions for particular states and conditions of life*.[3]

The emphasis in all these works was necessarily on personal devotion and on enhancing or creating a Catholic way of life. The post-Tridentine primer, and the early *Manual* were clearly intended for educated laymen, but a need was quickly realised for something simpler for the literate but less educated. As literacy increased at a popular level in the eighteenth century, the demand for such books increased and the possibility of inculcating a genuine personal devotion increased.

Gother's first devotional publication in 1689 began a series of small, cheap, devotional and instructional books, designed to meet the needs of every kind of Catholic.[4] The range of Gother's works indicates the social range of active Catholics in the late seventeenth and eighteenth centuries. Gother ranged from a prayer book designed to encourage active and intelligent lay participation at Mass, to instructions and daily prayers for masters, servants, apprentices, labourers, mothers, children, traders, prisoners, etc. Gother's works were the crystallisation of a growing tradition of personal piety in the midst of a distracting, unsympathetic, often hostile world. These books, the best missionary aid of the English secular clergy, initiated Catholics of the middle and poorer classes into a tradition of sober, penitential piety, grounded in their everyday lives, finding Christ in the world around them.

Clearly this was a tradition which produced the seeds of the Catholic revival. That sober, penitential piety among ordinary working Catholics was the means of sustaining English Catholicism into the nineteenth century. Generally speaking, it was a tradition which waned in the face of the nineteenth century Ultramontanism, though Gother and, more often, Challoner still have their devotees. In its time, it was a piety which had little to offend Protestant sensibilities and it found much affection among Anglicans of a High Church bearing, and was regularly adapted. It lacked the florid excesses of much of Counter-Reformation Catholicism and thus appealed to many High Churchmen of any generation up to the modern day, as being Catholic without being Roman.

Increasingly in the wake of Ultramontanism, recusant devotional life has come to seem cold, laboured and old-fashioned. Yet what could be more appropriate for modern devotional life than an emphasis on regular personal instructions, meditation and prayer, an emphasis on finding Christ in the marketplace, on making the whole of one's daily existence a prayer? Recusant spirituality, though in some ways a fossil, stands as a powerful challenge and a model of the most successful adult religious education programme ever attempted in England.

The second paradox under discussion is that of the relationship of recusant spirituality to the wider Counter-Reformation. It was at one and the same time peculiarly English and profoundly and formatively influenced by the contemporary European spirituality.

Anthony Wright, in his recent study of the Counter-Reformation, broadly follows the traditional view that the peculiar circumstances of post-Reformation England made the imposition of Tridentine reforms virtually impossible.[5] Episcopal implementation of Tridentine ideals was impossible where no real hierarchy existed, and where conflicts of authority were continued. He holds that surviving English Catholicism represented a continuation of medieval piety, with the retention of many pre-Tridentine forms of devotion (household devotions, fasting, holy wells, pilgrimages, etc.). This is partially true. certainly Catholicism survived very largely as a household religion in England, pilgrimages to holy places never really died out in the recusant period and, as I have indicated, recusant devotional works leaned heavily on borrowings from medieval texts.

However, it is by no means true that England was cut off from the Counter-Reformation in Europe. How could it be, when its priests were trained in Europe (albeit in English Colleges) and

97

most of its printed material came from European presses? The *Manual* itself leaned heavily on the works of Simon Verepaeus, one of the most popular and authentic Counter-Reformation writers, who aimed at reviving lay spirituality by means of publication of books of selected prayers and devotions.[6] However the really formative influence on recusant spirituality was Francis de Sales. The *Manual*, the *Key of Paradise*, Gother and, supremely, Challoner were all imbued with Salesian spirituality. The paradox and the achievement of the recusant tradition was that it created a distinctly English development of the dominant Counter-Reformation understanding of God, and man's relationship to God. It produced a form of Anglicised Salesianism.

The *Introduction to the Devout Life*, published in 1608, was translated into English in 1613. From then on Salesian spirituality, with its emphasis on the possibility and obligation of a fully Christian life lived in the world, was fostered in England. St Francis de Sales became the model of the English secular clergy, providing a distinctive alternative to the Ignatian spirituality of their rivals, the Jesuits. By 1630 Bishop Smith was urging Salesian devotion on clergy in training, and recommending the use of the *Devout Life* in their education of the laity.

As has been indicated, lay spirituality was dominated by a continual flow of small, cheap compilations of devotion and instruction. These all propagated a popular version of Salesian piety. It was rooted in the conviction that there was no way of life in which Christ could not be present. Sober, even a little grim in its tone, recusant devotion absorbed St Francis' emphasis on practicality and his democratisation of mental prayer. It was a spirituality wholly suited to the English temperament and environment, practical and ascetic, emphasising personal instruction and devotion and a Catholic life lived in the midst of everyday life. No other kind of Catholic life was possible for English recusants. It was self-denying and world-denying; prayer was presented as not merely possible but essential for Christians of all states, age and education; the business of the world was no excuse for its neglect.

Gother's work was the culmination of this spiritual tradition but the tradition now is associated mainly with Bishop Challoner. Many who have not heard of Gother have read Challoner and can see the influence of St Francis on him. Challoner's name is the one most readily linked with recusant spirituality, and if anyone from that tradition is still read, it is him, either *The Garden of the Soul*, or the *Meditations*. His devotional works are the embodiment of this English Salesianism and they rest squarely on the Gother tradition.

Challoner was confirmed and given his first Holy Communion by Gother, who was chaplain at the house where Challoner's mother was housekeeper. Gother trained and nurtured the young Richard Challoner's spiritual development and finally sent him to Douai to train for the priesthood. Challoner was the pastoral bishop *par excellence*, and was concerned with immediate and practical aims. His priorities were to create a body of sound secular clergy, who could preach, counsel and shrive, who were sober and obedient in habit and were distinguished not by wit or learning but by prayer. He expected from them the creation of the same qualities in the laity.

Part of his plan for creating the 'new people' which he prophesied was the production of a library of key books which would cover in a simple and straightforward manner the main aspects of Catholic life. He was dealing with a larger, less educated reading public, historically far removed from a pattern of daily Catholic life. He had to inculcate that pattern, as well as provide devotional material, and the task of writing was simply an extension of his pastoral concern. He did not write for the pleasure of intellectual pursuit, but to meet a pastoral demand. What he did has been described as 'Baroque devotion reworked for an age of reason, plain speech directed towards plain action'.[7]

His literary efforts were not original as Challoner had not a spark of originality in him. He devoted his energies to editing, translating and reworking older material, processing older texts (even in his own works) to provide plain and sober talk for plain men and women, while conveying the urgency of his spiritual vision. Instruction and piety to him were inseparable. His instruction always aspires to devotion and his devotional works are full of instruction.

The most famous and widely read of Challoner's works are *The Garden of the Soul* and the *Meditations*. So profound was his influence on the whole tone of English Catholicism that, until recently, anyone would have understood what was meant by 'a garden of the soul Catholic'; it was a Catholic strong in faith, solidly instructed, devout, with a deep interior piety, and a reticent, sober demeanour; the archetypal recusant. Both of these works blend instruction and meditation, in the tradition of the *Manual* and Gother, and are deeply imbued with the teachings of Francis de Sales, even containing direct borrowings. They have been described as 'simply his expression of the Salesian spirituality which had been fostered in England by the secular clergy for over a century'.[8]

The Garden of the Soul was first published in 1740, and went through thirty-four editions before 1824, equalling and surpassing the popularity of the *Manual*. Bossy, in *The English Catholic Community* asserts that the *Garden* was intended to supersede the *Manual* but he misunderstands Challoner's intentions. Challoner himself re-edited the *Manual*, and there was clearly a place for both books. They both run through a similar number of eighteenth century editions and the *Garden* clearly has a different intention, and is based on a different presupposition. Challoner did not presuppose any pattern of Catholic life and in the *Garden* his aim was to take the Catholic by the hand and initiate him into the way of spending his days as a devout Catholic. The *Garden* is much simpler, more basic, but it fits into the pattern of post-Reformation books of private devotion.

Challoner fitted into that pattern, but reworked it for his own rationalist, worldly age. He was an adapter and an adjuster retranslating the *Imitation*, the *Confessions of Augustine* and the *Devout Life* for his own generation, re-editing the *Manual* and *Ordo* and revising the *Douai Bible*. This further illustrates the paradox of a spiritual tradition very much of its time, yet with a timelessness which makes it perennially attractive, for Challoner's works helped to shape and mould Catholic spirituality for 200 years.

The *Meditations*, second only in popularity to the *Garden* in the eighteenth century, and still read today (by Lord Ramsey among others), was Challoner's most deeply Salesian work. It was published in 1754, containing practical instructions on the Christian Life, embedded in Salesian meditation and exhortation. Practicality was the keynote of the work and the meditations were not intended merely for study, but to be the seeds of pious affection for God.

The opening of the work is a treatise on meditation, and clearly spelling out the intention. 'The great truths of the Christian religion are here briefly proposed, in their own plain native colours.'[9] He recommends daily meditation of at least half an hour and gives a brief guide to affections which the pious Catholic may expect meditation to produce — faith, fear of the Lord, hope, love, shame and confusion, repentance and contrition, adoration, praise and thanksgiving, joy, humility, a desire to imitate Christ, compassion for Our Lord's suffering, abhorrence of evil. He is at pains to encourage the beginner in meditation, clearly aware that his instruction is the only form available. 'Mental prayer, by the way of meditation, is very easy, even to the meanest of capacities; it requires nothing but a good will, a sincere desire of conversing with God, by thinking of him and loving him. In effect, the great business of mental prayer is *thinking* and *loving*;

and who is there that can even live without thinking and loving?'[10]

Each of the meditations, for every day of the year and for the major festivals and seasons, has three considerations, concluding in a direction of the individual soul towards aspiration to God. It has a markedly liturgical character, partly because of its arrangement, and partly because the meditation for feasts and seasons usually takes the Gospel of the day as its text. This again reflects the way in which Challoner's devotional writings were not produced in isolation but were part of his whole pastoral endeavour. He was anxious in this to keep the Church's liturgical year before the mind of the individual.

The topics raised for meditation range over the whole field of doctrine, morals, ascetics, modelled closely on Francis de Sales, but with his own sombre emphasis on sin, death and judgment. Most of January and early February are given over to meditations on sin, all of July and part of August are devoted to death and hell. Sombreness of content and tone was a feature of Challoner's devotions and in fact the one aspect of the teachings of Francis which he could be said to have neglected was happiness or joy in God.

There is no mention in the meditations of the hardships of Catholic life; he writes almost as if oblivious of the distractions of social and economic disability, lack of clergy and chapels, poverty of community life. The only hardship to the Catholic in prayer is his own hardness of heart; with the right desire and will, the individual will create his relationship with God, and thus a new people shall come. The city over which Christ wept was not Christendom, or England or London, as well it might have been, but the individual soul. He points out briskly that time should not be wasted hoping for better times — 'This is your day; a time of mercy and grace', not a time of struggle and defeat.[11]

One of the most genuinely sympathetic judgements on Challoner and his importance as a devotional writer came from Ronald Knox in 1946:

> It was the age of the Encyclopaedists; chill blasts of rationalism threatened to stunt the development of spirituality. And Challoner, like his contemporary John Wesley, saw that if a religious minority was to survive, it must have a culture of its own. Like Wesley, he settled down with incredible energy to supply the lack himself, and formed by sheer application, the type of culture which is still, on the whole [in 1946] that of English Catholics, only leaving Faber to write the hymns. If we have since re-edited (for example) the *Garden of the Soul*, Challoner was the last

man who would, or should, have complained. He was himself, like Wesley, an adapter, an abridger, a continuator, rather than an original genius. In an age when nobody wrote badly, he was content, like Wesley, to write a great deal moderately, never giving himself time to write anything really well. We must have stock meditations for every day in the year, we must have the lives of the martyrs rewritten to a formula, we must have the *Jesus Psalter* purged of its old-world expressions, we must have our prayers stereotyped by a manual of devotions. The distant prospect of Emancipation was already in view; the tone, then, of English Catholicism must be English, must be cautious. There was to be no exuberance.[12]

That Englishness, caution and lack of exuberance deeply imbued lay and clerical education as it began to return to this country in the eighteenth century. The spirituality of Douai and St Omer was wholly the type of English Salesianism, which has been discussed, and it was deeply rooted in the lives of the secular clergy and therefore of the English schools and colleges which they founded.

The most important and influential lay schools which nurtured recusant spirituality in the eighteenth century were Standon Lordship (later St Edmund's) and Sedgley Park (now at Cotton). They were run by Douai-trained clergy (at one stage by two brothers, Hugh and Richard Kendal) and were preservers and adapters of the old tradition while creating new ones.

Religious training was central to life at Sedgley Park, and although intended primarily for lay education, it produced a large number of future priests. Bishop Milner, himself an 'Old Parker', called it the nursery of the English priesthood. Every day at the school began with a litany, reading and Mass, and on Sundays further readings were taken from Gother, read publicly after breakfast and before dinner. Daily evening prayer consisted of a litany and *Miserere*, examination of conscience, and a meditation from Challoner.[13] The spirituality of Sedgley Park was that of Gother and Challoner, inculcating in the boys a spirit of fervent love for the services of the Church, and strong habits of spiritual reading and catechetical instruction. Forms of prayer and liturgy were gradually expanded, particularly in the period from the late eighteenth century to the early nineteenth century when European devotions were introduced. Vespers and Benediction took place in the school chapel from 1801 and litanies began to be used regularly;[14] singing and the use of cassocks and surplices were introduced in 1805,[15] and local adaptations of Gother's and Challoner's prayers were produced. The festivals of the Church regulated the life of the school and the boys received Communion on the days of the Eight Great Indulgences, preceded by three days of preparation.[16]

These habits of piety and dedication were taken out into their homes and families by the pupils of Sedgley Park and, even more importantly, into chapels and congregations around the country. Many of the most active and influential clergy of the Midland District were products of Sedgley Park, so that the atmosphere and piety of the school affected the formation of numerous missions.[17] Among them was Bishop Milner, Thomas McDonnell, John Kirk, John Bew, Edward Peach, Thomas and William Southworth, Francis Martyn, Frederick Husenbeth and many others; they and the lay students apparently retained an extraordinary devotion to the school. Such was the rapidity with which recusant spirituality was superseded in the nineteenth century that Husenbeth, in his history of Sedgley Park, published in 1856, bemoaned the fact that the familiar spiritual reading of his childhood was no longer used at the school.

Challoner stands as the conclusion of a tradition of domestic piety which had begun to take root in the early years of the seventeenth century. It was a tradition which has produced no spiritual classics (with the possible exception of the *Garden*) and one which was rapidly usurped by nineteenth century Ultramontanism. It was so antipathetic to Ultramontanism that it was difficult for them to survive alongside. The *Garden of the Soul* has survived only because after 1830 it was edited to extinction, and became simply the vehicle for any compilation of prayers. For this reason, the spirituality of the recusant period and its devotional writings can seem uncannily remote.

Yet it has much to commend itself to us. It 'represents an authentic Catholic spiritual enterprise'[18] in which the great European movements in spirituality have been domesticated. The recusant generations adjusted and adapted Counter-Reformation spirituality to English needs and temper; there was a successful attempt to create a lay and clerical spirituality of genuine depth and piety and one based solely on the engagement of the individual with God by means of coherent meditation and prayer. As a spirituality produced by a religious minority in a pluralist and alien world, it has much to show us about renewal. The tradition of Challoner was finally jettisoned after Vatican II. In the haste for contemporaneity and renewal, the powerful combination of instruction and devotion was ditched; thus Challoner's *Meditations* ceased to be used regularly at Oscott in 1965. Yet, ironically, the recusant classics offer a wholly appropriate spirituality for modern man.

9

Two Russian parish priests

by
W. Jardine Grisbrooke

They had much in common. Firstly, by comparison with the majority of those considered in this book, they were both 'moderns': John of Kronstadt died in 1908, and Alexander Elchaninov, at a comparatively early age, in 1934. Secondly, they were both Russians: and I suggest that, quite apart from the personal spiritual help which they may be able to offer to some of us, they are significant and important precisely because they were Russians. Some insight into the thought, and the prayer, of two masterly exponents of Russian spirituality in recent times may make a valuable contribution to an understanding of what provides Russian Christianity as a whole with the impetus and the strength to survive, notwithstanding the determined assaults of the powers of evil against which it has now been in the front line of battle for seventy years.

Thirdly, both these men were Orthodox priests. Among the many tasks which face us in the search for the recovery of Christian unity, none is more important than the ending of the greatest, the most tragic and the most fortuitous and unnecessary of all schisms, that between East and West. Nothing is more necessary to the attainment of reconciliation than for each side really to get to know the other, not least at the deep level of spirituality. The writings of John of Kronstadt and Alexander Elchaninov are invaluable to the western Christian, Catholic or non-Catholic, in this context.

Fourthly, both these men were parish priests, and both were married. Neither the parochial clergy nor the married are well represented among those who are commonly recognised as outstanding teachers of the spiritual life, with the consequence that it is all too easy for the ordinary Christian, cleric or lay, to suspect, rightly or wrongly, that such teaching is neither addressed to his condition nor relevant or helpful to it. No such suspicion can be entertained for one moment about the teaching of these two men.

Fifthly, both were convinced adherents of traditional theology and traditional spirituality; and yet each in his own way was unconventional and radical. The reconciliation of the traditional and the radical is far from irrelevant to us today.

Finally, neither of these men ever consciously wrote a major spiritual work; they both kept spiritual notebooks, spiritual diaries as it were, which have deservedly become classics of spiritual writing. Most spiritual writing of value is the distillation of experience; these two books are pre-eminently and self-evidently just that.

John of Kronstadt's book, *My Life in Christ*, was published in his lifetime, and was translated into a number of languages. The English edition was published in 1897; it has, of course, long since been out of print.[1] It is a vast and (as might be expected from its origins) a totally disorganised work. Edited selections from it have been published on several occasions; the only one at present available is the volume entitled *Spiritual Counsels of Father John of Kronstadt*, edited by myself, published by James Clarke & Co in 1967, and reprinted in 1981.[2] Father Alexander Elchaninov's notebooks were published in English under the title *The Diary of a Russian Priest* by Faber and Faber in the same year, 1967.[3]

Father John of Kronstadt

John Ilyitch Sergieff, the son of poor peasant folk, was born on 19 October 1829, in the little village of Soura, in the province of Arkhangelsk in the far north of Russia. In his valuable work *A Treasury of Russian Spirituality*, Professor G.P. Fedotov characterises Father John as 'a genius of prayer'.[4] It is a perfect characterisation, and its first justification is to be found in its subject's childhood, for the young John Sergieff was very backward in learning to read. When he was nine, distressed at his backwardness, he gave himself to earnest prayer — rising during the night and praying while his schoolfellows slept — that this problem might be overcome; and overnight he found himself able to read well, and to understand what he read. It was a foreshadowing of what was to come.

He passed out top of his year from school, went to seminary, and thence, once more top of his year, to the theological academy of St Petersburg, for what we would call post-graduate studies. He was ordained priest on 12 December 1855, and was appointed to St Andrew's Cathedral, Kronstadt, where, first as assistant and afterwards as parish priest, he served throughout the fifty-three years of his ministry.

Kronstadt was a city which had arisen round a naval base on an island at the mouth of the river Neva, not far from St Petersburg, and it was largely composed of slums. To the inhabitants of these slums Father John gave pastoral priority, and the work that he did among them, both for their spiritual and for their temporal welfare, was quite extraordinary both in its total dedication and in its amazing fruitfulness. Like Mother Teresa's ministry in Calcutta in our own day, Father John's ministry in Kronstadt is a blazing witness against the falsehood of those who would set contemplation and action, prayer and practical work, in opposition to one another.

For Father John prayer and worship meant primarily *liturgical* prayer and worship, and he made it the centre not only of his own life and work, but also of the lives of thousands of his people. I quote from my own introduction to the *Spiritual Counsels:*

> He himself declared that only by partaking of the Body and Blood of Christ every day was he enabled to accomplish a task otherwise beyond human powers. When he came to partake of the blessed sacrament he would be utterly transfigured — all weariness, all burden of trouble and sorrow gone, and every line of his face reflecting an extraordinary spiritual joy, heavenly peace, and a great feeling of strength and power. Is it any wonder that his church was packed to the doors, Sundays and weekdays alike? The great cathedral of St Andrew at Kronstadt could hold 7,000 people, and when Father John celebrated the liturgy it was so crowded that, as a Russian saying has it, 'even an apple could not have found room to fall to the ground'.[5]

Two phrases in that passage call for particular comment. '. . .only by partaking of the Body and Blood of Christ every day. . .' It is difficult for us, 100 or so years later, to appreciate how radical, or revolutionary, was such frequent Communion. All over Christendom, in every denomination, infrequent Communion was the norm: most probably went to Communion but once, or at most three or four times, a year. The very idea of frequent Communion for the laity was thought to be spiritually dangerous. It was in that climate that Father John insisted that all who worshipped with him should also communicate with him every day. He was also concerned to arouse his congregation to more active and more intelligent participation in the service, in this too anticipating by many years the liturgical reformers of the twentieth century.

'. . .and a great feeling of strength and power.' None was ever more conscious than was Father John that the Sacraments are not magic. Time and again he points out that to be fruitful they demand faith and prayer. But, given that, if there is one thing that stands out in his teaching on prayer, as in his own prayer life, it is that he insisted on expecting results: strength and power. This to him was a vital part of faith, and essential to efficacious prayer. I will return a little later to this supremely characteristic and important aspect of his teaching.

Towards the end of his life, which coincided with a great period of spiritual revival in the Russian Church — not a little of it due, under God, to Father John — he constantly predicted in his preaching the approach of terrible times in his beloved Russia, a prediction which was to be only too completely fulfilled. He died early in the morning of 20 December 1908. I quote again from my introduction to the *Spiritual Counsels*:

> He who in this life cared so much for his children, and interceded for them so powerfully, has not abandoned them: the stream of healing, both bodily and spiritual, through his prayers has not ceased to flow. During the few years between his death and the catastrophe which he foretold, pilgrims journeyed to his tomb, and, although in the circumstances which have beset the Russian Church since 1917 it has so far been impossible formally to canonise him inside Russia, this final seal of the Russian Church's approval has been set on the devotion of the faithful to him by the synod of the Russian Orthodox in Exile, on 1 November 1964.[6]

'A genius of prayer.' Fedotov also says of Father John that his 'specific role was that of a *praying priest*'.[7] He understood all that he did, all that he achieved, as a manifestation of sacramental grace, fighting evil in all its forms. I have already commented on the absolute centrality of the Eucharist to his life and ministry. What is true of his life is true also of his teaching: it is marked by a clear insistence on the centrality in the Christian life of the ordained means of grace, and it is perhaps this above all else that marks him out as a sure spiritual guide for the ordinary man or woman trying to live the Christian life in the world, and for the ordinary priest trying to exercise a faithful and fruitful ministry in the world.

But Sacraments are not magic and, as already remarked, none has realised this more clearly, nor emphasised it more strongly, than did Father John. Fruitful reception of the Sacraments requires on the recipient's part faith and prayer. The two are intimately linked in his teaching: faith has to be prayed for, and prayer has to be based on faith. If one would learn about prayer, if one would seek encouragement in prayer, one could do a lot worse than turn to Father John of Kronstadt. His teaching on prayer is abundant, thorough, and eminently practical. Above all, it is clearly based on his own experience.

There is an awful lot of nonsense talked and written about prayer today. John Drury summed it up very well in a passage in his book *Angels and Dirt*:

> Someone I love is in trouble. Should I pray for him to get better? A sophisticated and somewhat patronising answer is that it can do no harm. It will calm me down and so, as a by-product, make me more comforting and reassuring in my dealings with my afflicted friends. That avoids the difficulty of suggesting that my prayer could make any real or mysterious difference, but it does so at the cost of saying anything at all vital or interesting about people or God. A double whisky might serve as well. It has also swept the whole question of asking under the carpet by substituting recollection in tranquillity, which is a different matter. This can be made more theological by making submission to God the object of the recollection. D.Z. Phillips, a contemporary philosopher, says that 'the prayer of petition is best understood, not as an attempt at influencing the way things go, but as an expression of, and a request for, devotion to God through the way things go'. This kind of enlightened view is sure to command respect . . .
>
> The majestic dignity of the enlightened view is enough to frighten us into accepting it. It is so much purer than the sort of praying which usually goes on. But it is not usually the best theology which captures its audiences by scaring them. That is itself a good reason for resisting it. Another is that the Christian tradition, in scripture and liturgy, contains a wealth of open and passionate asking, of people in particular adversity calling on God for particular help.[8]

To these modern 'enlightened' expositions of prayer and attitudes to prayer which, when carefully analysed, all too often reveal themselves to be no more than ways of emptying prayer of all meaning, ways of letting God and man alike off the hook, Father John's teaching on prayer, backed up as it is by his own experience of prayer and the evidence of the remarkable fruits of his own prayer, can be a most valuable corrective. He expected prayer to work; he expected results; and his prayer did — and does — work; he did — and does — get results. Prayer as strength, prayer as power: that, I think, is probably his most important message for us today.

His own spiritual life was of a kind to encourage others, for his was no sudden outburst of miraculous forces; his undoubtedly great powers of healing and of spiritual insight were the fruits of years of hard prayer.

Prayer — that was the key; and what prayer! His faith in prayer was tremendous. Two points above all others stand out from his teaching on prayer: the one, that prayer can achieve anything and everything; the other, that to do so it must be *real* prayer. He based his own praying on the divine promise: 'Ask, and you will receive'. He recalled constantly the pledge given in the incarnation: God, he maintained, who has given us a gift so infinitely surpassing any other, will not refuse the far lesser things which we need, and for which we ask. The dominant quality of his prayer — and this is as evident in his teaching as in the stories of his life — was power. At times he knew delight in prayer, but he did not seek it; and his prayer was far from disinterested — he desperately wanted something, and he asked for it, insistently, forcefully, indeed violently, taking full account of the Lord's words: 'The kingdom of heaven suffers violence, and the violent take it by force'. In his writing he constantly refers to answers to prayer, and repeatedly insists with an absolute conviction that it *is* worthwhile to act upon our Lord's promise: 'Ask, and you will receive; seek, and you will find; knock, and it will be opened to you'. Time and again he appeals, with total confidence, to experience (both his own and that of other people) as evidence of the efficacy of *real* prayer.

Of course, there is a great deal more to it than that, and were I writing at greater length I would be able to go into that 'great deal more'. As it is, I cannot, and it is probably just as well; I resist even the temptation to give some selected quotations. Father John's teaching on prayer is simple and clear; it is also, in its own way, a highly sophisticated, balanced and integrated whole, and it needs to be read, pondered — and prayed about — as a whole. I hope and pray that some readers of this book may be led to do just that.

Father Alexander Elchaninov

If Father John of Kronstadt is the most outstanding spiritual teacher of the Russia of the century before the revolution, Father Alexander Elchaninov is the most outstanding spiritual guide of the decades immediately before, during and after that shattering experience. He was a man eminently of his time, just as was Father John of Kronstadt, and he might well have been a man of our time also, for when he died, as the result of a tragically mishandled illness in 1934, he was only fifty-three. He was then at the height of his powers, and he could not unreasonably have been expected to have another twenty or even thirty years of active life and ministry before him.

Alexander Elchaninov was born in 1881, the heir of an historic family with a long military tradition. From his youth the extraordinary qualities of character and personality which were so marked in his later life were unmistakably present: he was already endowed with an uncommon attraction for other people, and a consequent unusual degree of influence over them. A former school-fellow, himself a man of no mean distinction, the late Professor Michael Karpovich of Harvard, said of him: 'It is hard for me to express how deeply I am indebted to him in my intellectual and spiritual development. I only know that fundamentally I owe more to him than to anyone else I have met in my life.'[9] And he knew him as a schoolboy.

Elchaninov read history and philology at the University of St Petersburg, and after taking his degree was offered an assistantship in the history department. His years at the university were years of considerable cultural and religious ferment among the intellectual classes of Russian society.

> It was a decade, says his widow in her introduction to the *Diary*, marked by a great recovery of faith, by a movement towards the Church on the part of circles in the Russian intelligentsia which had long been alienated from religion. In this spiritual revival the young Alexander Elchaninov himself played an active part: his university years already foreshadow the way of his entire life.[10]

A distinguished poet, who knew him during those years, spoke later 'of the unforgettable impression produced by this young student who, even in those days, represented ''the voice of conscience'' to so many of those whom he encountered'.[11] The extraordinary charm of his character played its part; as an eminent theologian, who also knew him at this time, said: 'When he appeared, with his gentle, luminous look, people's hearts went out to him, and a smile appeared on their lips.'[12]

Elchaninov early gave up his promising university career at St Petersburg, and moved to Moscow where, in addition to engaging in other academic and literary activities, he enrolled as a post-graduate student in the theological academy, although not with any intention of seeking ordination, which he does not appear to have contemplated at all. The study of theology and ordination have never been so almost invariably linked in the East as they have, to the Church's impoverishment, in the West. His course at the academy was interrupted by military service, and when the latter was over he did not return to the academy, having by this time strong misgivings about the value of the teaching there at that period. Orthodox theology, like theology in the West, was at that time dominated by a 'textbook' approach, and an arid neo- or rather pseudo-scholasticism, which owed more to the decadent schools of the seventeenth and eighteenth centuries than to the great flowerings of the golden age of scholasticism, and the neo-patristic revival was yet to come.

Instead, Elchaninov became a schoolmaster, and ultimately headmaster of a remarkable progressive co-educational independent high school in the Caucasus; incidentally, he married the daughter of the school's founder. He was deprived of his post as headmaster by the Communists in 1920 and all the progressive elements of the school's life and curriculum were, of course, eliminated. In 1921, like so many intellectuals, he was forced into exile. He settled at Nice in the south of France. After a period of teaching and lecturing, which might well have led, again, to a career of academic distinction, for the second time in his life he turned away from it, this time to seek ordination. He was ordained priest in 1926, at the age of forty-five. The same theologian whom I quoted earlier, who was also by this time in exile in France, and was influential in Elchaninov's decision to enter the priesthood, later wrote of his ordination that it 'led him to discover his highest gift and true vocation — that of a priest, a pastor of souls, a confessor and teacher. Every man is called to realise his highest gift: it was priesthood that revealed to the highest degree Father Alexander's interior strength and his power over human hearts.'[13]

When he died in August 1934, from complications ensuing upon a perforated ulcer of the stomach, Father Alexander had just been appointed Dean of the Russian Cathedral in Paris.

Father Alexander wrote a considerable amount but very little of it survives. The great bulk of his writing was in the form of occasional lectures and papers, many of which were never generally published; both the Russian revolution and the second world war contributed to an almost total loss of his unpublished papers and notes. *The Diary of a Russian Priest* contains notes that he wrote in the 1920s and 1930s (at the time, so far as we know, without any thought of publication), together with fragmentary notes for two books which he was planning at the time of his death, *Letters to Young People* and *Advice to Young Priests*. It is significant, and typical, that both those titles contain the word *young*, for he had always both greatly attracted young people and been greatly devoted to them, and during the later period of his life, both as a layman and as a priest, he exercised a remarkable ministry among them in the Russian Student Christian Movement in France.

His widow writes in her introduction to the English edition of *The Diary of a Russian Priest*:

> Apart from these chapters [containing the notes for the two proposed books], planned by the author himself, the rest of the material is presented without any systematic order; this has been done deliberately, so as not to offer any interpretation that might stand between the reader and the author. Each reader is left free to discover for himself, according to his own needs, what was the essence of Father Alexander's spiritual image.[14]

She also points out (and if one is to use the book with profit, as well as to get an accurate picture of its author, it is important to heed the warning) that

> ...being composed of random notes, the book naturally does not represent every aspect of Father Alexander's character. Most of his notes are concerned with ascetic themes and with problems of the spiritual life, and as a result they may convey a certain impression of severity, which was not in fact at all characteristic of him. He was, on the contrary, lighthearted and full of radiant joy, indulgent towards the faults of others, natural and spontaneous, with a subtle irony and humour.[15]

What Tamara Elchaninov says of him is fully confirmed by many others who knew him.

Professor Fedotov who, as we have seen, characterises Father John of Kronstadt as 'a genius of prayer', similarly characterises Father Alexander Elchaninov as 'the teacher of self-examination',[16] and says of him that:

> . . . with a distaste for the use of any force whatsoever, he simply opened to those under his guidance the way to self-examination. And he himself was a master of the technique of self-examination. Perhaps this is his real vocation in the spiritual life: he is not a struggler or a mystic, but a serene and kind counsellor, meek but interiorly austere, a stranger to any kind of opportunism.[17]

It is hardly surprising that the private notes of such a master of spiritual direction, read outside the context of a living contact with his personality, 'may convey a certain impression of severity': he takes the problems of the spiritual life, and in particular the problems of sin, seriously. But if they are read as what they are, if they are read remembering all the time what they are, there is much in them of great value.

There is another aspect of Father Alexander's life and teaching, another factor in the development of both, to which I would call attention, both on account of its importance for understanding and appreciating him (and especially because of its contribution to that 'certain impression of severity'), and on account of its relevance to the state of the world in which we ourselves live today. I quote again from Fedotov:

> The harrowing experience of the Revolution and the destruction of all hope for the peaceful cultural development of Russia produced in Elchaninov, as in so many others, a profound reaction . . . Theirs was the apocalyptic attitude of mind which characterised the early Church and the Fathers of the desert.[18]

This is indeed typical of Russian spirituality in the twentieth century, whether inside Russia or outside it, and I doubt whether anyone who has had more than a merely minimal acquaintance with that spirituality has remained untouched or uninfluenced by it, or unaware of its vital place in a truly Christian attitude to ourselves and to the world in which we live. It would, I suppose, be dismissed, totally inaccurately, as 'pessimism' by the practitioners of the facile, superficial and essentially worldly 'optimism' which disfigures too much of western spirituality today, an attitude to which *The Diary of a Russian Priest* can be a valuable corrective and antidote.

But there is another aspect, too, of Father Alexander's spirituality which at times comes to the fore in the *Diary*, its principal themes notwithstanding. The note of Christian humanism is only muted, not lost: the experiences of the last seventeen years of Father Alexander's life did not kill his belief in, and hope for, the possibilities of Christian intellect and Christian culture, nor did they diminish his deep appreciation of beauty, both in nature and in human artefacts, and of human love and friendship. Far from it: the value of these things stood out all the more against the background of evil and destruction.

In this, especially above all in his love of the beauties of the natural world, and his awareness of their witness to their Creator, Father Alexander was at one with Father John of Kronstadt. He was at one with him in much else too, and among it, interestingly, in his desire for liturgical reform: there are several passionately outspoken passages on this subject in the *Diary* which anticipate by several decades what many others have since said, but not often as trenchantly. (Whether either of these pioneers would in the event have been happy with much of what passes for liturgical renewal today is, perhaps, another matter.)

So far as their published writings are concerned, however, it would be possible, by partial interpretation admittedly, to suggest a marked contrast between the two men. A cynical and snide critic could, by such means, caricature Father John's teaching on prayer as 'God's in his heaven, and all's right with the world', and Father Alexander's teaching on sin as 'God's in his heaven, and all's wrong with the world'; and I would not deny that there are passages in both of them which do tend to give this impression, if they are read out of context and in isolation both from their authors' lives and from the rest of their teaching.

But the fact is that neither 'God's in his heaven and all's right with the world', nor 'God's in his heaven and all's wrong with the world' is true, or even partially true, if it be said in isolation from the other; and both are true, wholly true, if they be taken together. I would suggest that the two great masters and teachers of the spiritual life considered in this chapter were so partly, at least, because they both realised, far more acutely and far more completely than do most of us, that paradoxical truth, and because they lived, and prayed, and worked, with far greater understanding of it, and greater commitment to it, than do most of us.

One who knew Alexander Elchaninov well once said of him: 'The most essential thing is his simplicity. Not the primitive simplicity of a man unacquainted with the world's complexity, but a far-seeing simplicity that has taken the measure of that very complexity.'[19] The same could, I think, be said of John of Kronstadt, for all that he was a very different man, from a very different background, who led a very different life and exercised a very different ministry.

That simplicity is the simplicity which can at one and the same time lay hold of the truth of the warning in the early Christian writing called the Epistle of Barnabas that 'those who desire to see me shall pass through tribulation and despair', and the assurance of that great English mystic, Mother Julian of Norwich, that 'all shall be well, and all manner of thing shall be well'. May God grant us all a measure of that simplicity, which is but a reflection of his own.

10

The spirituality of the English Catholic modernists

by
John Berry

This is a brief study of the spirituality of two English Catholic Modernists: Baron Friedrich von Hügel (1852-1925) and Fr George Tyrrell (1861-1909), with a passing reference to the thought of their friend and collaborator Maude Petre (1863-1942).[1] Each of them expressed a deep personal commitment to the dimension of the Church's tradition which is indicated by the word 'spirituality'. They were concerned to explore that aspect of the Christian life where belief, prayer and practice come together in human experience. Their stated desire was to elucidate that point of our lives where faith and reason, mysticism and morality, belief and practice are gathered up and find expression in the prayer and worship of the Church. They sought vigorously to recover the depth and diversity of the Catholic spiritual tradition and to enter into the theology and practice of prayer in order to apply it creatively to the needs of Christian believers in a changing culture and society.

Of course they were deeply interested in questions of biblical criticism, historical research, the development of dogma, the theology of revelation, and the nature of the Church and its teaching authority. But it is possible to claim that the central interest binding the modernists in England was a desire to reassert the fundamental place that prayer and spirituality must occupy in the life of the Church and in the life of each believer. They were sharply critical of what they felt to be the dry, arid, abstract and rigid spirituality they had experienced, and it represented for them a quite defective system of thought which had come to dominate official Roman Catholic theology. This view was shared by continental thinkers such as Blondel, Laberthonnière, Le Roy, Bremond and Loisy. They were all united in their intention to replace this whole framework of thought. However much their 'programme' had undoubtedly negative and destructive consequences, its original intent was, in part, a genuine search to restore some of the neglected elements of a rich, spiritual tradition. They sought to relegate what Gabriel Daly has called 'supernatural rationalism' in order to rediscover the 'interior, living, mystical source of all true religion'.[2]

The modernists inherited an ecclesiastical world which had been shaped by several factors: the condemnation of Quietism in 1699 and its aftermath, the influence of Jansenism, a strong conservative political and social ideology, the triumph of Ultramontanism, and the increasing dominance of a form of scholasticism which owed more to Suarez and other interpreters than to St Thomas himself. The consequences of the dominance of this school were a deep suspicion of such concepts as 'experience', 'intuition', 'heart', 'affection', and 'feeling' in reflecting on Christian life and faith, and a real hostility to *le fait intérieur*. A rather narrow 'intellectualist scholasticism' certainly exerted a theological hegemony in the Catholic Church at the time von Hügel and Tyrrell were beginning to write. It was eventually reinforced with the full weight of authority in 1907 when Modernism was officially condemned. But at the turn of the century they were both striving to re-establish a uniquely 'spiritual theology' in which these suspect categories could be fully embraced and positively integrated.

In Tyrrell's opinion the prevalent popular moral and spiritual teaching led in practice to a starving of the affections, a stultifying of the emotions and a resulting distortion of spirituality. The negative, unimaginative spiritual maxims circulating in manuals of piety and volumes of ascetical theology had been inculcated in the rigidly-disciplined atmosphere of the seminaries with certain unhealthy consequences.[3] He spoke from personal experience as a confessor, retreat-giver, spiritual guide and preacher with some knowledge of schools and seminaries, and parishes as different as St Helen's and Farm Street. His indignation was directed against those who were happy to perpetuate the prevailing system, those whom he castigated as offering nothing more than 'temporary palliatives' to deal with the 'spreading epidemic of unbelief'.[4] He could be biting and caustic in criticising the 'Pharisees and Logicians', the exponents of 'priestcraft, clericalism, Jesuitism and Vaticanism'.[5]

One sad practical consequence of this dominant system was the inability or unwillingness to integrate the Church's rich heritage of spiritual theology. When that heritage had been taken up he felt it had often been misused and misapplied. Thus, 'unwary and unstable souls had been warped and perverted by the *Imitation of Christ,* John of the Cross and the *Spiritual Exercises.*[6] It was the whole tradition of which these were a vital part that both he and von Hügel sought to recover and integrate with what they felt to be recent insights in theology and even the emerging behavioural sciences and research in comparative religion. Both agreed with the programme set out by Loisy: 'to renew theology from top to bottom, to substitute the religious spirit for the dogmatic spirit'.[7] This conviction was born of Loisy's personal experience, having encountered the 'chilling effects of rigid dogma on spiritual experience'.[8] Maude Petre felt able to write of the modernist enterprise as part of a battle between two distinct schools: 'the apparent opposition of the orthodox and strictly dogmatic expression of religious truth to its spiritual meaning.' Significantly, it was chiefly von Hügel who managed to hold together the vital importance of dogmatic truth and mystical truth both in his religious philosophy and his own life.

Von Hügel especially, but also Tyrrell, represented the very opposite of the narrow, ecclesiastical closed mind. Their meeting and friendship, which is evident from their voluminous correspondence over a period of twelve years, grew from a common desire to explore the Church spiritual tradition. As Barmann put it, von Hügel was attracted to Tyrrell 'because of the latter's penetrating and discerning emphasis on the more mystical aspects of religion within a church whose official emphasis had become, he thought, too centred on scholastic rationalism, and the external, structural aspects of religion.'[9] His *Mystical Element of Religion* was an attempt at a synthesis in which spirituality assumed its central place in religion. His life-long task, as he expressed it in many letters and in his published works, was a renewal of Christian spirituality out of its roots in tradition and based on a perception of contemporary needs. As he wrote in the preface to his *opus magnum*: 'More than ever the spiritual life appears now as supremely worth the having'. His study of Catherine of Genoa, John of the Cross, and the mystics in general, and their relation to Christ himself, was undertaken to stimulate life and love and to spur others on to 'fuller religious insight, force and fruitfulness'.[10] Although researchers in modernism have not always adverted to it, this 'pastoral' or spiritual motive was uppermost in the minds of both von Hügel and Tyrrell. The Baron was looking for 'a synthesis of Sanctity and Science, in the Church and for the Church'.[11] In this remark one can also see another characteristic of the Baron's approach, his fundamental loyalty to institutional religion, a fact which prompted Loisy to call him 'the true Father of the Church, the true Augustine'.[12]

That Tyrrell shared this understanding of the modernist enterprise is evidenced by his description of the apologetic task: to 'connect the truths of theology with the truths of history and science', and his statement that this was to be an 'affective apologetic which appealed to the will and affections by enlarging on the beauties and the utilities of religion'.[13] Tyrrell is not above the charge of a certain undiscerning naiveté in speaking of a reconciliation of theology with the 'assured results of science', and he is best understood as articulating an angered and sometimes irrational and extreme reaction to a narrow, scholastic theology which seemed to take little account of the impact which science was having on intellectual culture in general and which he felt had also become divorced from spirituality and lived experience.

In his attempt to draw from the well-springs of the Christian spiritual tradition Tyrrell the Jesuit was naturally attracted to the charism of St Ignatius Loyola as one possible way to help renew contemporary spirituality. This found expression in the desire to discover the authentic spirit of the *Exercises* beneath the alleged 'accretions' of the 'theological logicians'. Though he never fulfilled his ambition to publish a new and helpful edition of the Ignatian *Exercises* the constant hope itself illustrates his abiding concern to present spiritual teaching in a form which would meet the needs of Christian believers experiencing a world in transition. This genuine motive reflects his basic fidelity to his priesthood and the needs of the faithful. Whatever the faults of Ellen Leonard's account, she was right to stress this aspect of Tyrrell's efforts: 'The focus for Tyrrell's work was not that of the scholar, as in the case of Loisy, but of the spiritual director. His interest was religion, devotion, the spiritual and mystical life'.[14] It is significant that his earliest and quite traditional works of piety, *A Handful of Myrrh* and *Another Handful of Myrrh*, which originated as parish talks (though he later described them as his 'least loved progeny')[15] were the result of his desire to bring out of the Church's store both 'new and old', and to present truths which might speak to a changed and changing situation. His many introductions to and editings of the spiritual classics and lives of the saints are also an eloquent testimony to this concern, and to his popularity as a communicator. Von Hügel admitted in the Preface to the second edition of *The Mystical Element* that his own vast study of mysticism owed a good deal to Tyrrell's profound knowledge of the history of mystical theology.

On reading both writers one begins to sense more and more that they had an abiding devotion to this spiritual tradition and that, despite so many other influences, they had been deeply formed by it. They sought at every opportunity to present it again to the whole Church. So much of their scholarly labour grew from the attempt to seize this whole tradition from the grip of a narrow school of official theology and to allow it to live again, and become a means to a reform and renewal of the Church's life and theology.

Experience: our meeting place with God

The theological context for the modernist attempt to renew Christian spirituality was a recurring debate about the relationship between divine transcendence and immanence. Gabriel Daly has observed that von Hügel 'regarded the question of divine transcendence as the most crucial issue in the religious thought of his age'.[16] Loisy thought him obsessed by it, mocking the Baron's notion of a 'gendarme metaphysique', and Maude Petre saw it as the main reason why he distanced himself gradually from other modernists.[17] The Baron became ever more sensitive to the dangers of a one-sided stress on divine immanence, a fault he perceived in Tyrrell at one stage when he spoke of the latter's over-emphasis on God's Immanence at the expense of the 'Areopagite insistence on Transcendence'.[18] He criticised Tyrrell for his failure to express this vital truth:

> If one were to take your clear-cut Immanentism as final and complete, that noble half of the religious experience of tip-toe expectation, unfulfilled aspiration, of sense of a Divine Life, of which our own but touches the outskirts, would have no place.[19]

But two years after Tyrrell's death von Hügel was able to write of Tyrrell's continued stress on the transcendence of God in the face of growing immanence among the rising generation of scholars. So by this stage the Baron was claiming that in Tyrrell's opposition to a 'purely immanentalist answer or analysis' and his assertion of transcendence, 'I was heart and soul with him'.[20] Transcendence had always been essential to the Baron's understanding of the Christian mystery. Although he could accept Blondel's 'method of immanence', employed as part of a broad attempt to link man's contingent nature with the abiding reality of the transcendent God, he could not tolerate a reduction of the 'old transcendent conception of God' in the interests of an immanental one since this represented not only an over-simplification but a radical impoverishment both theologically and spiritually.

What von Hügel offered was a 'rich middle position' between the two extremes of Exclusive Transcendence (which, he said, became in the hands of the scholastics, a 'tyrannous Transcendence') and Exclusive Immanence (which for some modernists had become simply 'sceptical subjectivism'). Von Hügel found the balance not merely in terminology, speaking of 'immanent transcendence', but in his whole scheme of philosophy and mystical theology. For him, what is encountered by man is the immanent presence of the utterly transcendent God. He was fond of speaking of friction and tension, polarity and paradox in elucidating his spirituality. The dynamic of man's spiritual life reflects the alternating activity of God himself, the Transcendent who is ever immanent because always revealing himself.

> The uncompromising Transcendence and the compromising Immanence, the intense touch of God the Supernatural, and the genial dilution of it within the human nature which, in its essential qualities and needs, is good and comes from him, are both necessary and closely interrelated in our Christian call and work.[21]

Whatever the similarity between this and the scholastic use of the term 'transcendence', von Hügel's understanding of the reality is living and dynamic, a Transcendence that is ever immanent, felt, sensed, and touched in human experience.

It is at this point that we can observe one of von Hügel's most striking contributions to the Church's spiritual tradition: his insistence on the centrality of human experience as the place where God meets man. The human has become the indispensable locus of divine communication. It is worth noting that 'experience', as von Hügel used the concept, became an even more suspect notion in Roman Catholic theology after the condemnation of Modernism in 1907. For von Hügel it was a vital element in his developed Christian anthropology with its positive awareness of man's bodily nature and the role of the senses and emotions in the apprehension of reality.[22] In holding together the cognitive and conative ways of knowing, the Baron was clear that the apprehension of God springs up on occasion of one's consciousness of the finite. The world of bodily sense impressions, where the cumulative gathering of disparate experiences of reality occurs, is the ineluctable place where the individual comes to a knowledge of God. Thus, 'Spirit is awakened on occasion of Sense when Sense responds to stimulations from Realities other than itself', and it is Catholicism alone, von Hügel maintained, which stands fully for this 'great fact of Spirit *and* Sense, Spirit *in* Sense, Spirit *through* Sense.'[23]

One important consequence of this approach is that there is no place for any separate mystical or spiritual *faculty* since it is in the depths of one's total experience that the transcendent God becomes immanent and is encountered, loved and adored. In his discussion of *Experience and Transcendence* the central question von Hügel addressed was 'how can man, the Finite and Contingent, solidly experience the Abiding and Infinite?' In seeking to meet this question he asserts the existence of an 'immense and all penetrative force throughout human life', and a sense of contrast between 'the changing, penetrating, stinging sense of the relative and finite', of the 'merely human' with the 'contrasting other'.[24] But the latter appears and is grasped on the occasion of the former and this fact is absolutely central for von Hügel. What is mediated through the matrix of life is a 'direct and universal, though dim, experience of God'.[25] Patrick Sherry has given a succinct summary of this aspect of the Baron's thought: 'For von Hügel, religious experience is mediated through our overall experience'.[26]

It is in relation to this whole question of transcendence and immanence that a contrast between von Hügel and Tyrrell is apparent. Though the Baron's final judgment of Tyrrell in this regard was positive there is no doubt that a distinct difference of emphasis is discernible in their approach. And so, despite the truth in Ronald Chapman's remark that Tyrrell's contribution 'is to be found in the attempt he made to reconcile "transcendentalism" with "immanentism" ', his emphasis falls quite definitely on the *immanence* of the divine which, though only dimly knowable, draws man towards a higher plane, the level of 'Infinite Subjectivity'.[27] Tyrrell stressed 'mystery as a necessity of life' and dwelt constantly on the fact of 'mystery' in his theology and spirituality and, although he did not insist as strongly as von Hügel on the sheer transcendence of God, he was drawn, nonetheless, to similar conclusions about our experience of divine immanence. The role of mystery, then, is to entice us into the 'cloud of unknowing' where the divine is felt and experienced at a level deeper than the intellect alone. Always prepared to point out the failures of 'narrow, cock-sure orthodoxy', with its clear-cut catechism answers, Tyrrell criticised those 'to whom everything is clear and commonsense, and obvious, who can define a mystery but have never felt one'.[28] This was reminiscent of Blondel's criticism of some of the less able exponents of scholasticism who saw things too clearly to see them well.[29] Our apprehension of the divine is always mediated, dim and obscure, as 'in a glass darkly', a scriptural phrase Tyrrell was fond of repeating. Thus religious truth will never be other than mysterious, since revelation and mystery are two names for the same reality: 'Eternal truth is revealed to us in so far as God gives us a twilight glimpse of the rough outline, of some little corner of the picture here and there'.[30] And here is the essence of his belief that revelation must be understood primarily as experience.

Though one notices a shift of perspective from the young to the older Tyrrell culminating in the radical programme of *Christianity at the Crossroads*, he seems never to have lost this deep sense that our meeting with God in this life will invariably be 'dark', 'dim', and 'shadowy', in a 'cloud of unknowing'. Here he was at one with von Hügel and the apophatic tradition of the Christian spiritual writers, the *via negativa* of the Church both in the East and the West. The intensely personal note of all Tyrrell's writing is nowhere more evident than when he speaks of the darkness of faith, and an early meditation entitled *Gleams in Darkness* captures this in his attractively lyrical style:

> 'Stay with us for the night is failing.' Remain with us, for the dark is coming in; that darkness and black night which recurs in our soul, if not as regularly, as surely as that night which inevitably follows on the day. He is with us, then, and we may hear his voice; though we can see his face but dimly, if at all, nor can we discern his movements. And yet at such times, perchance in the Breaking of Bread, he flashes in upon our soul in a way that we never knew in the time of light — a sudden recognition Dominus est — 'It is the Lord!' and then he vanishes, leaving us in darkness, but in peace and joy.[31]

Five years later, when his interior struggle had begun to dominate his whole life, he wrote from his personal experience of this darkness, and revealed the element of resigned 'intellectual agnosticism' which marked his whole spirituality: 'I am content to be much in the dark; perhaps I prefer it, as God seems nearer'.[32]

Tyrrell's stress on experience, with its doubt and darkness and its inevitable interior struggle, governed his understanding of revelation which he conceived not as intellectual statement but as inward experience of the indwelling Christ, 'the inward stimulus and attraction towards the divine'.[33] If, then, this divine action and stimulation be the very substance of revelation, the way God speaks to us, our response must be obedience and devotion, not merely ethical but 'religious and mystical'. Taking up Matthew Arnold's idea, Tyrrell suggests that what we experience is a 'Power making for Righteousness', 'a Spiritual will drawing our wills into union and relationship with himself'.[34] This gave rise to Tyrrell's idea of conscience as 'the voice of the whole that is immanent in us as in its parts'. This union of wills reminds us that man in this way 'lives a divine life and rises above his own relativity'. It is through the matrix of human experience that the God of mystery penetrates humanity and reveals itself. In this sense God is always met as the immanent One. In man's response, for Tyrrell as for von Hügel, adoration is central in our response, though he insisted more than the Baron on the ethical component of the human response. Thus, 'man always and everywhere feels that there is something in the unseen world he must worship and obey'.

For stressing the 'interiority' of religion Tyrrell was charged repeatedly with 'immanentism', and though there is little doubt that he accepted the *method* of immanence in principle it would be difficult to maintain that he ignored transcendence completely in the interests of an absolute *doctrine* of immanence. Rather, Tyrrell recognised that, in Daly's words, 'all human thought is centrifugal and that God cannot bypass this fact of human nature'.[35] It might be more accurate to say that God *does* not, rather than he *cannot*. If one asked which part of man comes most fully into action in religious apprehension, Tyrrell would answer with the word 'feeling', as he does throughout *Religion as a Factor of Life*. Despite the suspicion of official theology he took up the word feeling, central to the immanentist emphasis, and utilised it in his discussion of the human will and the heart as the place where God's presence is experienced. To some the word represented a dangerous capitulation to sentimentalism, subjectivism and emotionalism. But for Tyrrell it served to denote the 'sense of the Absolute' mediated in human experience as the first impulse to religious interest and commitment. Schultenover clarifies this important point: 'To say that religion is a matter of felling is to say only that religion controls the mainspring of life', though this is not to say that it is the whole of life. It is quite as acceptable to speak of religion as sentiment or affection as it is to call it beliefs or good works, since the locus of religion is the 'internal will-attitude rather than the perception that precedes or the action that follows.'[36]

So Tyrrell's conclusion was that Absolute Reality (what von Hügel would always insist on calling the Transcendent) was not merely one element among many in the world of objects but the abiding and underlying Reality which pervades and permeates the whole of our experience. Thus, 'the Infinite sheds its rays as though in a "luminous mist"', in the Ideal, the True, the Good and the Fair though its form and nature lies shrouded in mystery'.[37] Since he was often charged with voluntarism and subjectivism it is to be noted that Tyrrell understood grace as operative precisely at this point where man's whole spiritual and physical nature is touched and elevated by the power of God's presence. Something of a dialogue takes place between Absolute, Transcendent Reality and limited, finite human personality. In a crucial passage Tyrrell parallels the statement of von Hügel quoted earlier: 'the sense of the Absolute is given not beside but *in* and *with* and *through* the sense of the Ideal in every department'.[38] The term 'spirituality', then, may be used to describe the heart of religion, since it is the relationship in which God calls forth from within man a life that is 'latent and buried — the life of personal communion with Himself, the strength of self-conquering love.'[39] Tyrrell was unwilling to lose hold of this truth about the essential 'inwardness' of true religion, and it was manifest even in his final and most radical work *Christianity at the Crossroads*, where he stated that the 'idea of Jesus as the Divine indwelling and saving Spirit seems to me the very essence of Christianity.'[40]

This notion of 'indwelling', signifying the depths of God's involvement with the human heart, was a theme taken up by Maude Petre, Tyrrell's friend, biographer, disciple and literary executor, in three volumes produced at the height of the modernist period.[41] She shared with Tyrrell a basic modernist outlook and commitment to Blondel's 'method of immanence', and took up other familiar 'modernist themes'. She spoke of God working in the human heart in practices of piety and devotion but also as inspiring and permeating our actions in every sphere of life. Statements such as 'it is in ourselves that He is to be found' were always likely to arouse the critical opposition of official orthodoxy invariably suspicious of the human heart, feeling and interiority as appropriate categories for theological reflection.[42] This is not to deny that it was never quite clear that she was avoiding a total subjective immanentism. But Maude Petre persisted in her fidelity to the 'modernist cause' right up to her final years even when for many the issues had been well and truly buried. In her autobiography published in 1937 she wrote that if we submit to the guidance of intuition, rather than mere rational knowledge, we begin to see 'some kind of identity of each of us with the life that comes from, and that, is a sense, is God.'[43]

Mysticism and the practice of prayer

If the spirituality of the believer is seen not as an esoteric realm into which only a select few are admitted, but rather as everyday life in all its spiritual depth and richness as the place where God's presence is experienced, then prayer and mysticism are to be understood as 'ordinary' or 'natural' in the sense that they too are rooted in everyday human experience. Writing to Algar Thorold in 1921, von Hügel claimed that 'not only all Science, but especially all knowledge begins with intuition — a certain mysticism, if you like.'[44] But he was also clear that mysticism required other realities for its active existence, what he called 'historical happenings' and 'social religion'. It is this insistence on the elements of religion that is most often associated with the thought of von Hügel. It is the context for his understanding of the phenomenon of mysticism.

In the first volume of *The Mystical Element of Religion* von Hügel establishes his scheme for understanding religion as it expresses itself in history and in the individual. The three elements 'as they successively appear in the Child, the Youth, and the Adult Man', are 'three modalities, three modes of apprehension and forms of appeal and outlook', which are at work within and around us. They are: i) sense and memory, or the child's way of apprehending religion; ii) question or argument, or the youth's mode of apprehending religion; iii) intuition, feeling and volition: the mature man's approach to the faith. So, mysticism belongs to our mature practice of religion, where we come to know our true self and experience a growth and deepening of our personality. At this point all dimensions of the person, emotional, volitional, ethical and spiritual powers, are in full and harmonious motion as they are fed by the experiential and mystical realities of life. Now 'religion is rather felt than seen or reasoned about, is loved and lived rather than analysed'.[45] It is important to note that von Hügel does not seem to be speaking of a simple chronological progression here; rather, 'the three stages must be seen not as successive but as cumulative'.[46] The central element, however, will always be the mystical.[47] Von Hügel was also clear that although institutional religion was his 'hair shirt', it was also the proper context for myticism. By insisting on a definite connection between the philosophy of critical realism and Christian mysticism, he asserted a position which involved a critique of what he claimed to be Troelstch's misunderstanding of the mystical element of religion.[48] At the heart of mysticism is 'intuition', the 'sense of the Infinite which engages all the dimensions of the personality and which cannot be located exclusively within any 'mystical' or 'spiritual' faculty. His view was that the insights of the Catholic mystical tradition were confirmed, not undermined, by contemporary thought in general and a critical realist epistemology in particular. His own philosophical analysis of human experience had revealed the 'sense of the Infinite' in which the non-discursive faculties played a full and active part. Thus he highlighted sensation, feeling, volition and particularly this 'intuition' which he regarded as 'the most indispensable and truest form of experience'.[49] This crucial word *intuition*, closely related to his use of the word *sense*, seems to have been an inclusive umbrella term which identifies and indicates the perfected or intensified operation of all the human faculties working in fruitful harmony. To dwell on Christian mysticism, is thus to be taken back to experience as the locus of our deepest spiritual encounter with God. Sherry again provides us with a lucid summary: 'For von Hügel "mysticism" is simply experience of God'.[50] Mysticism consists of plumbing the depths of our ordinary but complex experience and exploring to the full the sense of the Infinite that we discover there.

During his period at Farm Street Tyrrell, too, became pre-occupied with similar questions and in 1897 found himself deeply concerned with a series of questions raised by Henri Joly's *Psychologie des Saints*. Again, it was in mutual exploration with von Hügel that he was able to articulate a clear position in answer to the question 'what is mysticism?'[51] In dealing with the suggestion that mysticism is a natural and ordinary phenomenon which is simply an intense experience of God, Tyrrell began by recognising the real difference between those who prefer to keep saints at a distance as simply extraordinary, and those who find something common and universal in all sanctity. If one rejects the idea of mysticism as illusion or visions or extraordinary physical phenomena, and sees it primarily in terms of the experience of love (Joly defined it simply as the 'love of God'), then the ordinary Christian differs from the saint 'not in his mysticism but in the degree of his mysticism'. So the saint is only intelligible to us in so far as there is a real continuity between our 'inceptive love' and his 'perfect love', a sameness of kind between the seed and the flower.[52]

Clarifying his position in a letter at this time he stated: 'I like the insistence on a certain continuity between the lowest and the highest degrees of sanctity, and the recognition of the elements of mysticism in even the most rudimentary forms of divine love'.[53] This view of mystical experience also accepted positively 'feeling' and 'tactual intuition' which, Tyrrell admitted, fitted uneasily into 'scholastic psychology', yet further proof that the latter had become so unrealistic as to be no longer serviceable. His conclusion is brilliantly concise: 'If love be mysticism then we have the key to all mysticism within ourselves'.[54] It was a conclusion shared by von Hügel who held that mysticism existed 'in some form and degree, in every mind. Only in its intensity and extension, in its quantity and quality will it then differ in various souls'. It is a conclusion that is also remarkably contemporary, finding an echo in a modern writer on mysticism: 'Mystical experience is a profound realisation of what we are and of the grace we already possess'.[55] For this reason, to seek an understanding of mysticism and mystical knowledge one must begin with human experience and the nature and destiny of human beings created in the image and likeness of God.

Within the modernist movement both von Hügel and Tyrrell were regarded as deeply spiritual men and seen to be drawn personally to the mystical dimension of the Christian life. This view has also been maintained by others. Writing of von Hügel, Lester-Garland noted the 'fervent intensity' of his spiritual life which 'shines through all he wrote'.[56] Maisie Ward said of him, 'he was a saint and a mystic as much as a scholar and a thinker'.[57] Von Hügel's judgement of Tyrrell is interesting: 'You are a mystic: you have never found, you will never find, either Church, or Christ, or just simply God, or even the vaguest spiritual presence and conviction except in deep recollection, purification, quietness, intuition, love'. He spoke of Tyrrell's 'deep great spiritual life which is your one strength'.[58] Maude Petre identified several characteristics of Tyrrell's thought, one of which was 'a profound spirit of mysticism'.[59] When von Hügel and Tyrrell spoke of mysticism and the practice of prayer they did so from personal experience of the spiritual journey, the constant struggle to remain on the pilgrimage of faith. Here the element of autobiography is closely bound to their theological reflection.

Turning directly to the place of prayer within this 'modernist spirituality' one finds their thought intimately related to their basic theme that the dim sense of the divine presence is encountered not beyond or 'outside of' but *within* human experience. In sensing the Infinite man does not stumble aimlessly from one insight to another, floating on a sea of vague sense-impressions with no thread of continuity. It is at this point, at least for von Hügel, that the mystical element merges with his concept of prayer and recollection which takes place in the recesses of the human heart where the experience of the immanent Transcendent is appropriated and dwelt upon. For the Baron, prayer is an exercise in assimilating and absorbing, recollecting and unifying such experience. It is from such 'states of recollection' that the soul moves outwards again 'to love, to work, and suffer for God and man, beyond its previous level'.[60] Prayer is thus a vital point of growth in the whole of life, a crucial element in the dynamic movement which marks the Christian life in the spirit.

Von Hügel spoke in personal terms to Wilfrid Ward of this alternating movement of prayer and action at the heart of life; it is a movement of the mystical mind from the 'centre of intense light' to the area of 'twilight' and the darkness, and then the return from such weary 'borderwork' to 'sink back upon its centre, its home of peace and light'.[61] There is no gulf envisaged here between 'ordinary life' and some 'religious' or 'spiritual stratosphere'; rather, the whole of life in its bodily-spiritual reality is the locus of prayer and recollection. Tyrrell clearly assented to this: 'I am cordially with you when you say 'Religion and life are one and the same; for I hold religion to be the culmination of life; i.e. of man's self-adaptation to his environment'.[62] As von Hügel put it, the stimulations affecting man from without contribute to spiritual growth and 'it is in recollection and solitude that he assimilates them'.[63] For the religious person, prayer must become an abiding reality in life, ensuring cohesion and stability amid the diverse movements in day to day living. Prayer is the dynamic, integrating element in this process of personal growth and the most intense and fruitful form of action. In a homely image the Baron instructs his niece in the simple necessity of prayer:

> . . . the great rule is, variety up to the verge of dissipation; recollection up to the verge of emptiness: each alternating with the other and making a rich fruitful tension or friction. Thus we gather honey from all sorts of flowers, then sort out, arrange, unify and store, the honey gathered. After which we again fly out on our honey-gathering expeditions.[64]

And this basic 'prayer disposition' must 'penetrate all one's waking hours'.[65] In this way he saw his niece's 'continuous openness to the impressions (fresh as ever) brought you by all things beautiful and true and good' as a great gift, 'a form and kind of deep faith — a true prayer'.[66] What the Christian is seeking is not clarity but richness, not cleverness but fruitfulness; and fidelity to practical love and authentic prayer are means to these ideals. Prayer, for the Baron, is undoubtedly a 'costing task' at the heart of which is *adoration* as the first and most spontaneous response to the sheer *isness* of God. But prayer is not adoration alone; it is also reflection and recollection, working to integrate the touches of God on my life; it is also intercession, the movement out from myself towards God, in Himself and others.

In two substantial addresses delivered in 1921, von Hügel laid the theological foundations for his understanding of prayer. From the record of these talks, *The Facts and Truths concerning God and the Soul which are of most importance in the life of prayer*, we can only note some of the emphases which make von Hügel's spirituality a significant contribution to Catholic tradition.[67] Following, he believed, the inspiration of Fénelon, he asserted the fact that God is *the* transcendent, rich Reality, and the consequence that 'not even Jesus Christ and his redemption exhaust God'. Seeking to avoid a one-sided 'Christocentrism', he sees prayer as taking us beyond the humanity of Christ into the very life of the Triune God — the deepest Reality of all. Nonetheless, God is reflected in his creation and nature, and so is always the 'dim background of our lives'. Further, God alone is fully free and has given himself to us, and so 'our prayer will be immensely enriched and expanded by a persistent cultivation of the sense of God as our true home'. This demands a depth in our lives which can only become a reality through the constant practice of prayer. God is the living Source of all life, the Transcendent Other, and our Sole True End, and these truths determine the nature of our prayer as primarily adoration, though petition, contrition and thanksgiving must never disappear from our spiritual lives. Finally, the 'prevenience of God' is a truth at the root of all other truths about God, and one which ensures a depth and vitality in our prayer. The Baron felt that these key facts, if held together, would bring 'much depth and breadth, much variety and elasticity into our prayer'.

In the second paper the Baron shifted his perspective to view prayer in its relation to the bodily life of man, beginning with the connection between prayer and life. In practice, what is required for each human task is balance and single-mindedness, leisure and flexibility. Prayer is no exception. Dryness and aridity in times of prayer may simply reflect dissipation and a drifting life outside prayer; and this is a fact of life, a consequence of man's nature as a complex psychosomatic unity. Accepted in this spirit, such 'desert stretches', such states of dryness and darkness, are 'irreplaceably profitable'.

Moving on, the Baron then accepts the old truth summed up in Abbot Chapman's maxim: 'pray as you can, and not as you can't', though he gives it a fuller rendering in his treatment of another favourite term, *attrait*. Since each human being is a unique individual, von Hügel can accept wholly 'the great difference, in spiritual range and depth, in special *attrait* and peculiar calls and gifts, unchangeably inherent in each soul's vocation to what it is, and still more to what God would have it become'. He quotes with approval Fr Faber who, after describing the Ignatian method of prayer, exclaimed: 'thank God it is not the only way to God'. He was expressing the basic truth that spirituality is not a strait-jacket but the growth of our own individual personality through the interpenetration and integration of all our traits of temperament and character. The way God leads *me* will be precisely his way for *me*. To undergo the transformation God wants of me I must become 'saturated with prayer, by the spirit of prayer, vocal, mental or of quiet'. Von Hügel's own recitation of the rosary, at the suggestion of his director Abbé Huvelin, anchored him in the first and simplest and most humble form of prayer, and his fifteen minutes' spiritual reading each day and eucharistic adoration rooted him firmly in the traditional sacramental spirituality of the Church.

This brings us naturally to his next important 'fact': this sense of the Infinite and the prayer it inspires has a social, communal context in an organised Church. Indeed, the Church itself has the specific task of the 'awakening, the training, the bringing into full life and fruitfulness of the Supernatural life'; this it accomplishes through putting us in touch with the Risen Christ. This reminds us of the central importance of the sacraments as expressions and celebrations of God's love for us, and also illustrates the core reality of Catholicism, that 'Christ everywhere makes use of the sensible to convey the spiritual, never the spiritual alone'.

The fifth of the 'seven facts' in von Hügel's scheme centres on the need for a right attitude to the sexual instinct and the insistence that the virtue of purity is a fleshly virtue which does not deny but directs this God-given instinct. In this connection it is pointed out that 'the central sin, for the Christian, is pride and self-sufficiency, distinctly more so than impurity and sloth'. This leads him on to assert the importance of adopting a right attitude in general to sin and temptation which can be seen, certainly in the tradition of St Augustine, as the occasion for 'a grand humility and for the keenest sense of the mercy of God'. The final 'fact' stated by the Baron is the need for a large and deep asceticism in the life of prayer: 'the Divinely intended End of our life of joy, overflowing and infinite, a joy closely connected with a noble asceticism'. Both von Hügel and Tyrrell accepted the traditional truth that there is no mysticism without asceticism, and much of their spiritual counsel in this area is profound and moving. Joy is also rightly understood as a mark of Christian living, but when austerity is practised it too becomes 'an integral constituent of all religion'. The traditional terminology of the ascetical tradition, cross, mortification, self-denial, suffering and sacrifice, is clearly present in their letters of direction, and real personal suffering, in different forms, was part of their own experience of the Christian way. Von Hügel believed that devoted suffering was 'the only quite pure form of action'. Both of them spoke with impressive conviction of the centrality of the cross in the Christian life. The Baron spoke of his 'white nights', and darkness and aridity in his spiritual life and Tyrrell's own journey was marked by a particularly intense experience of anguish, emptiness and darkness.

When Tyrrell wrote of prayer he too located it firmly within our bodily life and experience. On one occasion he used an image similar to that of the Baron in his letter to his niece. He spoke of the bee alternating between the cell and the flower-world, gathering in and building up new matter so that its home hours may be more fruitful. Similarly, man pieces together 'an ever fuller image of God from the fragments of Divinity scattered among creatures', and the more he is able to do this, the 'easier and more fruitful will his prayer be'.[68] He felt that contemplation which was unrelated to the activity of ordinary life could easily weaken or impoverish those very faculties in the exercise of which prayer consists. True prayer, mystical or contemplative, has nothing to do with the 'delusions of visionaries', or the 'extravagances of agnostics, Neo-Platonists, or even Christian mystics'. Neither is it 'morbid quietism' or 'a complete deadening of the affections and stupefaction of the mind'. Nor is it pure subjective spiritual experience. It is 'that love of God without which no soul can put forth the blossom of its highest perfection and salvation'. So, the 'ineffable union is not the privilege of a few elect souls, but an obligation binding upon all'. It is clear how closely linked this is to the whole discussion of mysticism. Tyrrell felt this form of prayer and devotion was more important than ever in a time of rationalism in theology which tended to 'dry up the springs of tenderer devotion'. This was one reason for his insistence that devotion must guide theology, and the key to his belief that the *Lex Orandi* is inseparable from the *Lex Credendi*. Theology that makes one pray less is bad theology. He points out that in Catholic tradition the rule of prayer has had a privileged place in the evolution of belief and doctrine.[69] Knowledge of God can never be the concern of the intellect alone. Thus, prayer, in the rich and wide sense in which Tyrrell used it, is a means to deeper knowledge of self and God. The great aim of the spiritual life and any form of prayer is to 'enrich the significance of the word God'. This may appear a little uninspiring as it stands but what Tyrrell means is that true prayer leads us from a mere notional or formal realisation that God is, to a real, experiential sense of his presence and his power in our lives. This is achieved by actually tasting and loving 'His sweetness as shared by creatures' who reflect the 'scattered rays of Divine Beauty'.[70] There is nothing here which permits a remote 'other-worldly spirituality' unrelated to God's presence in his world and in his people. Though a gift, prayer remains the activity of man who is incarnate spirit.

Since Tyrrell's spirituality is 'earthed' in this-worldly reality, there is, as with von Hügel, an insistence that prayer takes place within the body, and is in no sense an escape from material creation, or a denial of its goodness. On the matter he makes a point of contrasting Christianity with Buddhism: 'we must not be like the Buddhist contemplative stupefying our minds even to the bare consciousness of existence, but remembering that God has made all things good and god-like in some degree, we must ascend from the likeness to the original'.[71] As with von Hügel there is a decisive rejection of any 'mystical faculty'.

What we may call the 'incarnational principle' was a strong element in the thought of both von Hügel and Tyrrell, and an especially important foundation principle in their theology of prayer. Tyrrell was at pains to elucidate what this meant in practice. In saying that we pray but also God prays in us, and that we pray to what is within us as well as what is outside us, and that prayer is always creative, Tyrrell maintained that 'the first and most essential characteristic of true prayer is *reality*'.[72] Developing this theme he became more disposed to accept the role of darkness, doubt and tension, and the challenge that prayer offers to all our familiar conceptions of God. He learnt through bitter experience the truth of Eckhart's statement that 'man's last and highest parting occurs when, for God's sake, he takes leave of God'.[73] Writing from Fribourg, in April 1906, he referred to his own anguished trial in recovering the living prayer of the Breviary: 'One has to pass through atheism to faith; the old God must be quite pulverised and forgotten before the new can reveal Himself to us. Patchings and mendings have an end; and revolutions are heralded by periods of chaos'.[74] Ultimately, prayer will dispose us to withdraw our attention from all else and 'turn it upon our relation to God'.[75] This is dedicated, single-minded prayer through which my own interest merges with God's interest. This is not magical prayer, nor is it a violation of human nature. It is the 'sane mysticism of the gospel'. So, the spirit-life is essentially supernatural and mystical, but it is also a 'strengthening and perfecting of the natural or psychic life'.[76] As with von Hügel the heart of Christian spirituality is the practice of prayer, which is the indispensable way to growth and fullness of personality.

Conclusion

It would require a considerable amount of time and space to assess accurately the modernist contribution to spiritual theology since it would involve relating the writings of von Hügel and Tyrrell to the whole spiritual tradition of the Church. What cannot be doubted is that they were both well acquainted with many aspects of that tradition, and displayed a genuine respect for it. A few concluding remarks will simply hint at how one might begin to assess their place in this dynamic of tradition.

Von Hügel was steeped in the Catholic tradition of spirituality from the patristic period to the post-Tridentine French tradition to which he became particularly attached. For him it was, above all, Fénelon who embodied this part of the tradition, bearing witness to 'a Catholic piety, wisdom and experience of life'.[77] In terms of individuals, Grou was a trusted guide, and Mabillon the scholar-saint was also an exemplar, combining piety and scholarship in a manner which appealed strongly to the Baron whose instinct drew him towards a deep commitment to both learning and sanctity. He also recorded his personal debt to two contemporary priests, Hocking and Huvelin, who had helped and guided him. In addition he revealed to his niece a deep reverence for the 'grand old pre-Reformation Catholic piety of England'.[78]

Tyrrell, too, had a keen interest in the roots of Christian spirituality, revealing especially a love of Mother Julian of Norwich and the medieval English mystical tradition. But neither von Hügel nor Tyrrell was simply digging around for some 'golden age'; rather they were seeking the roots for a renewed spirituality in the rich heritage of undivided Christendom and the tradition preserved beyond the Reformation. Von Hügel was happy to draw from the Church's diversity, from the 'heroic monastic' and the 'homely domestic' aspects of her life and history, but he did not want to be rigidly confined within any particular one.[79] Nédoncelle noted the Baron's failure to observe obvious connections between different saints, writers and schools of spirituality but conceded that this failure may be beneficial since it 'brings home to the chroniclers of the mystical life the need for caution in mapping out a general theory; and in this respect his silence is a lesson'.[80] Despite the Baron's clear limitations, such as his tortuous prolixity and heavy, ponderous style, it is difficult not to find his presentation of spirituality stimulating and valuable. Heaney's conclusion is admirable: 'one cannot read him without coming away with a deepened sense of God and of the spiritual life'.[81] Perhaps in the long term his contribution is to be seen in his general description of the manner of God's involvement with man in the world and in human experience; quite simply how God becomes accessible to human beings, and what this demands of us. Evelyn Underhill saw his originality in terms of his deep consciousness of the 'close-knit texture of realities within which we live and move'.[82] This opened the way for a spirituality which recognised and affirmed the presence of God in and through every aspect of his created world.

As regards Tyrrell, in pursuing personally the spiritual path, and writing of it often in prose of 'limpid beauty', he had to contend with what he called his 'imperfect psychic "chemistry" ', and the 'hopeless tangle' of his life.[83] This in a sense points to one aspect of his appeal as a spiritual writer. As Ronald Chapman put it, 'Tyrrell became one of those rare people who are as much at home in the strange seas of the human psyche as on the dry land of everyday fact'.[84] His passion for 'the real', his fear of 'illusion, pretence and sham', gave to his writing a dimension of sheer honesty and integrity which, some have felt, is often not quite as apparent in von Hügel's life and writing.[85] Gifted as a spiritual guide, Tyrrell's spiritual theology was rooted in the realities of life, and his acceptance of doubt, darkness and the pain of belief as integral to true prayer has retained a strong appeal. Describing his life as 'the travails of an Irishman in search of a Religion', he wanted to produce some reflections on the analogy of 'how to live on sixpence a day', entitled *How to live on the minimum of faith*.[86] The amusing self-deprecation in this and other remarks touches the heart of Tyrrell's pathos. The complexity of the man is also suggested by a contrast of images: the 'tired, wistful, determined' Tyrrell 'wandering restlessly' in the darkness of the small hours of the morning on Clapham Common', and Tyrrell immersed in the regular daily round of study and prayer in the Jesuit house at Richmond in the magnificent Yorkshire Dales. Tyrrell in personal spiritual anguish and Tyrrell enjoying an expansive restful peace: two threads of a complex, enigmatic tangle.[87]

Whatever inconsistencies and errors may be found in von Hügel and Tyrrell as modernist theologians and writers, their insistence on a wholesome and affective spirituality as a central and abiding dimension of Christian life and thought should ensure them a place within the spiritual tradition of the Church. In terms of a possible foundation for a twentieth century spirituality in a Church proclaiming a universal call to holiness it would be difficult to ignore them without risking the loss of valuable insights. But there remain misgivings. Tyrrell's excessively negative view of the danger of a dominating dogmatic spirit rendered him less capable of appreciating the crucial value of doctrinal statements as articulations of truths which can foster prayer and serve to draw us into the mystery of God and his revelation. Von Hügel, despite the appearance of compartmentalising, was rather more successful in holding together in tension the positive function of dogma and the inarticulate striving of the human heart, the essential complementarity of dogmatic and mystical truth. The precise achievement of von Hügel was to retain a vision of the indispensable interrelation of the three elements of religion in which the exclusion of any one would have been not only an impoverishment but a destruction of true religion. In the characteristic emphases of both von Hügel and Tyrrell one can sense the potential for a combination of mysticism and 'materialism' where the latter is understood in terms of Incarnation of God in Christ. One can sense too the possibility of a legitimate *panentheism*, seeing God above all things yet in all things, and also a wider, deeper and more realistic understanding of the dynamism of personal spiritual growth.[88]

The period from 1890 to 1910 saw the emergence and growth of what became known as the modernist movement. Von Hügel and Tyrrell were, without doubt, part of that intellectual ferment in Europe which absorbed the Church at the turn of the century and beyond, and consequently their distinctive contribution to the Church's spiritual tradition, though flawed by their heterodoxy in other areas, has too often remained unnoticed or even denied. At the height of the modernist crisis when the condemnation of the 'compendium of all heresies' was issued, von Hügel and Tyrrell were, significantly, deeply immersed in a highly technical and rigorous study of the central questions of mystical theology. In Tyrrell's view the Baron's study of the mysticism of St Catherine of Genoa was 'a great vindication of the reality and religious depth of "modernism" '.[89] It is even possible to re-interpret the modernism of von Hügel and Tyrrell as a concerted but, in the end, abortive attempt to revive mystical theology in the Church and for the Church. In this way it may be thought to reflect, however opaquely, a more widely diffused and complex revival of mysticism within the Church at the time. Significantly the same period produced mystics and saints whose lives and teaching have proved to be of enduring value for the Church in the twentieth century.

Whatever the limitations of the prevailing spiritual theology God's gift of holiness is constantly offered and received. Contardo Ferrini (1859-1902), Elizabeth Leseur (1866-1914), Hieronymus Jaegen (1841-1919), Gemma Galgani (1878-1903), Charles de Foucauld (1858-1916), Elizabeth of the Trinity (1880-1906) and

Thérèse of Lisieux (1873-1897) are simply the most striking examples of this mystical revival.[90] In the case of the last three their contribution to the renewal of the Church's spirituality and mystical theology has been of immense significance, relating especially to the centrality of the sacraments and the Eucharistic presence of Christ, the immanent indwelling presence of the Triune God in the baptised believer, and the place of the mystical vocation of love within and for the *whole* Church. These characteristic emphases, which are being reappropriated by the Church and which will endure beyond the present century, are not entirely unrelated to the concerns articulated and explored by von Hügel and Tyrrell. At another level one may also note that the 'mystical question' which became such a pre-occupation for certain theologians of the present century such as Poulain, Arintero, Garrigou-Lagrange, de Guibert and Marmion on the continent, and Chapman, Butler, Knowles and others in England, had already received considerable, persuasive and imaginative treatment at the hands of von Hügel and Tyrrell.[91] In this light it is difficult to resist thinking of them both in terms of Abbé de Tourville's perception that 'in every age God has scattered forerunners in the world. They are those who are ahead of their time and whose personal action is based on an inward knowledge of that which is yet to come'.[92]

11

A note on contemporary spirituality

by
Kevin McDonald

This series of essays has offered an introduction to some of the most influential writers in the Christian tradition. The Desert Fathers, Walter Hilton, St John of the Cross all continue to speak to us today. But they inhabited very different worlds from the one we inhabit, and it is important to bear this in mind as we read them, and as we seek nourishment from them. We cannot seek union with God in medieval England, or Counter-Reformation Spain, or nineteenth century Russia. We can only seek God from where we are, from within the world as it is, and with that self-understanding that is ours, simply because we live in the closing decades of the twentieth century.

The purpose of this note is to draw attention to some people and some developments which are representative of prayer as it is practised and reflected on today. The writers I will mention are authors who speak to us in the language of our time. I want first, though, to note some of the features of our world and our Church that distinguish them from the Church and the world of previous centuries.

The setting for prayer today

Those of us who live in Europe — the home of most of the writers mentioned in this series — are aware today of the existence and condition of peoples who live thousands of miles away from us. The world is a smaller place. In particular, the suffering and deprivation of the poorest people in the world have been brought home to us in a way that is quite new. We are aware of the unjust economic system that perpetuates the gulf between rich and poor countries, and our sensitivity to justice and human rights is very much a feature of this age. Victor Codina in an article in *Concilium* in 1982[1] argued that for prayer to be authentic it must be prayer in solidarity with the poorest people on the earth so that, today, the prayer that is pleasing to God is prayer that issues from a heart that is concerned about the real evils and injustices we live with.

A further point about our western society is the amount of stress people live under. Material prosperity and sexual liberation have not removed human anxiety; they may well have heightened it. Some of the best spiritual writers are those who have accurately diagnosed the condition of men and women in modern industrial society and are able to speak of the fear and loneliness that we all share in some measure. Ours is also a secularised society; religious commitment is the exception rather than the rule, and many of those who seek God seek him in very real isolation, without the support of a definite doctrine or of a Church community.

The Church too has witnessed major upheaval in modern times, and the developments that have taken place since the Second Vatican Council have affected the prayer of Catholics profoundly. There has grown up a positive openness to other Christians, to other religions and to the secular world. We are not afraid to learn from other Christians and to be enriched by their theology and practice. We now take very seriously the tradition and practice of meditation in the Eastern religions. We also recognise that the activity of God is not and cannot be confined to the visible Church. In particular we see those who work for justice and human rights as caught up in the activity of God in the world. Within the Church itself, the liturgical developments of the last twenty years have had a marked effect on the way people pray. Most obviously, personal prayer may now be guided and enriched by the liturgy in ways that are only possible when the words of the liturgy are understood.

Good contemporary spiritual writers — and I will outline some examples — must be those who have their hand on the pulse of the modern Church and the modern world. Their popularity lies in the fact that they resonate with people's experience: they nourish people as they are and where they are and are in that sense genuinely contemporary.

An inner journey

A life of prayer is a journey; a journey towards deeper union with God. It is also an inner journey, a journey within oneself. Many contemporary writers in the field of philosophy, of religion or comparative religion tend to see mysticism, prayer and contemplation as essentially the same process in all religions: all that varies is the doctrinal interpretation put on the same experience. Writers like Erich Neumann see mysticism as an essentially therapeutic process which unifies and integrates the consciousness.[2]

Disagreeing with this point of view does not mean seeing the findings of contemporary psychology and philosophy as a threat to the reality of Christian prayer. Rather, we may see them as illuminating the nature of the inner journey that a Christian undertakes.

This is the case for H.A. Williams and Hugh Lavery. Although very different from one another, we may take them as good examples of Christian thinkers who are profoundly affected by the age in which we live. Both write in a vein that would have been inconceivable before Freud. Both have successfully touched the nerve of people's loneliness and anxiety and are able to put those things in the wider context of faith. In his book *The True Wilderness*, Williams wonders how we are to understand the biblical image of the wilderness, or the desert, today.[3] He concludes that we find the wilderness within ourselves. It is within himself that man experiences fear and isolation; isolation from those who are more happy and successful than oneself, and isolation even from those who are physically closest. But, as in the Bible, there is a reason for being in the wilderness:

> To feel isolated, to be incapable for the time being of establishing communion, is part of our training. That is because so far our communion has been shallow, mere pirouetting on the surface. We've come to see its superficiality, its unrealness. Hence the feeling of loss. The training doesn't last forever. In fact, new powers of communion with our world are being built up within us.[4]

Hugh Lavery talks frequently in his essays about people's anxiety and sense of guilt: he sees these things as inevitable in a world of 'unfaith'. Not being able to believe in God means not being able to accept that we have a loving Father, and in that situation we cannot experience the gratitude that goes hand-in-hand with faith. And we are all affected by this, believers and unbelievers alike. Lavery says we are anxious because we question God's care and God's competence: we cannot really bring ourselves to believe, and that is the sin of our age: unfaith. This is a characteristic piece of Hugh Lavery's writing:

We cannot speak to our contemporaries only in terms of the quest that engages them. Freedom is now the deep desire. In the last century it was political; the vote was vital. Now, economic freedom means salvation, and affluence is the answer. Yet, strangely, freedom remains elusive. And it is now seen as Jesus saw it, as an interior thing and as a relationship. Autonomy is not viable; no man is an island. A man lives and grows through relationships and the deep relationship is with God. But how can we know God, feel God, relate to God? This is the oldest question, the only question. Jesus answers 'I am the way'.[5]

A writer who embarked on the spiritual journey and has encouraged many to do the same is Thomas Merton. It is clear from his autobiography, *Elected Silence*, that he felt all the tensions that are typical of this age, and he took them all with him into the heart of traditional Christian monasticism.[6] His interpretation of Christian doctrine is at the same time an interpretation of his own condition, and this is the secret of his power as a writer and teacher.

Merton says that because of Original Sin, man is exiled from God and that means that his state is one of exile from his true self. Man is born into what is essentially a world of illusion and the purpose of the life of prayer is to undergo a transformation in which we come to find our true selves. And the things we have to go through on the way — emptiness or defencelessness or solitude — are all inevitable in the process whereby the old self gives way to the new.

A person's new self — his true self — is a self that is totally united with God in love, but without being absorbed into God:

> the union between the soul and God in love is close and so complete that the only remaining distinction between them is the fundamental distinction between two separate substances . . . the only trace of distinction that remains between them is the fact that what is God's by nature is the soul's by participation, and by God's free gift, that is by love.[7]

The point is that man's authentic existence is the state of love and the life of love that are the fruit of union with God. Sin means remaining in inauthentic existence. Prayer, therefore, is in no way an escape from life and from responsibility: it is not simply an altered state of consciousness, sought in the pursuit of greater happiness. Rather, in discovering our true selves, we are able to take responsibility for ourselves and for others. To the extent that we have not undergone this transformation, our work in the world will be to little real effect. All we will communicate to others will be our own aggressiveness, ambitions and obsessions.

East and West

The inner journey that our authors speak of has been substantially illuminated by the dialogue between Christianity and non-Christian religions. Some of the most intriguing spiritual writing today comes from the pens of Catholics who have gone to India and Japan and become very personally involved with Hinduism or Buddhism, for example Bede Griffiths, the Benedictine monk who has lived in an ashram in India.[8] Another — and the one I wish to focus on — is William Johnstone[9], a Jesuit from Belfast who twenty years ago took a doctorate at Sophia University in Tokyo. Since then he has been living in a community that comprises Buddhists and Christians, and his books, which are modern classics of Christian spirituality, are the fruit of this encounter with Zen Buddhism.

Johnstone maintains that Zen gives Christians a much-needed technology for deeper and simpler prayer; we need not be afraid of drawing on its technique of securing concentration and tranquility. Just as the early Church both assimilated and rejected elements in Greek culture, so must contemporary Christians in their contact with the East. He says that the comparative failure of Christian evangelisation in the East may have been because of Christianity's failure to be receptive to local culture and local religion.

So how are the traditions of East and West to meet and nourish one another? Johnstone says that sharing and unity are realised between Christians and Buddhists when they meditate together, and not when they talk. The Zen masters say that words are like fingers pointing to the moon: we must get beyond words. In discussion we will find that Buddhists do not share our belief in a personal God, but Johnstone is convinced that the best way to negotiate our divisions is to share in meditation. Both Christian and Zen meditation are concerned in different ways with personal transformation with the growth of love and compassion in the personality. Zen aims at completely overcoming any sense of being a subject confronting an object; those involved in Zen meditation seek to be released from their ordinary rational state of consciousness, and to reach the point at which all is one. This is done by techniques that hinder rational thought and which open up the deeper layers of the human spirit to establish that state of enlightenment at which everything is one; that oneness or enlightenment is the object of Zen meditation. Clearly this is something very different from Christianity. But Johnstone says 'Zen monism reminds Christianity of the unity of all things and of our oneness with God'. In Christian meditation we do not seek the dissolution of the self in order to become part of the One; what we do seek is to become one with the universal cosmic Christ whose glory fills the whole earth. Christian theologians have spoken of God as the 'ground of our being'; what Zen can illuminate is the inner journey, deep within ourselves, towards the ground of our being. Johnstone frequently refers to the great mystics in order to show that this is precisely what they were doing: leaving the world of rational conscious thought, to find God in the deepest part of themselves. This explains, for example, why St Teresa described the soul as an interior castle which has a series of mansions that must be gone through if we are to reach the centre of the castle, where we will find the King. And Johnstone refers to passages from St John of the Cross, such as this one where he describes his own experiences:

> Sometimes mystical knowledge absorbs the soul and engulfs it in a secret abyss; the soul is placed in a most profound and vast retreat to which no human creature can attain, such an immense desert which nowhere has any boundary, a desert the more delectable, pleasant and lovely for its secrecy, vastness and solitude wherein the more the soul is raised up above all temporal creatures, the more deeply does it find itself hidden.[10]

Christianity is not about losing one's identity, but it is about dying to oneself. Johnstone says that dying to self and appropriating the new life of Christ is a process that is most lucidly expressed in St Paul's words: 'I live, no not I, but Christ lives in me' (*Galatians 2:20*). What William Johnstone's books are about is how that can become a reality.

Like Thomas Merton, Johnstone affirms that meditation is not an escape but is rather the most influential and powerful of human enterprises. Christ is at work in the world, restoring all things to himself, and the person who has arrived at unity with Christ in the depths of himself has been caught up in God's saving activity in the world. Such a person humanises the world in a way that no one else can. Unenlightened social action will not bring the love and compassion of Christ into the world. This becomes especially clear in what Johnstone has to say about friendship. Unity with Christ brings with it a capacity for unclinging friendships, unclinging because they issue from a heart that harbours real love and compassion for the whole of human nature and human society.

Renewal in the Spirit

The importance of Christianity's encounter with the East is beyond dispute. Apart from anything else, it has brought renewed stimulus to rediscover our own mystical tradition. Arguably, though, it has distracted attention from some of the more characteristic themes of Christian spirituality: imitation of Christ, conversion, repentance, etc. Whether that is the case or not, it is important that what has come from encounter between East and West be set against the fruits of the meeting between Catholicism and evangelical Protestantism that has taken place within the West itself.

Charismatic renewal began as a revival movement within American evangelical Protestantism. The movement made its impact on the Catholic Church in the early 1960s in university campuses in America. It has spread throughout the Catholic world and has made a profound impact on Catholic life and worship.[11]

The concern of those involved in charismatic renewal, as of those Christians involved with Eastern religions, is that people should experience the reality of God in their own lives. Christianity is not simply a matter of fulfilling certain precepts and rules; it is about the renewal and conversion that God wishes to bring about in each one of us. The particular characteristic of the movement is the insistence that all Christians should claim the promise of the Father by being baptised in the Holy Spirit. Christ promised the gift of the Spirit to those who believed in him, and so we may ask the Spirit to come down on us as he did at Pentecost. Often the Baptism in the Holy Spirit is given after a series of preparatory seminars. Those who have already received the Baptism in the Spirit then lay hands on the person seeking it and pray for him. Sometimes the effects of this prayer are immediate and dramatic; as the Spirit is released, so are the gifts of the Spirit, such as prophecy, teaching, tongues and healing. People are given gifts which then form the basis of their Christian life and ministry. The gifts are received for prayer and for service in the Church. The two gifts that have attracted particular attention are the gift of tongues and the gift of healing.

The gift of tongues is not unusual as a manifestation of Baptism in the Spirit. The person finds himself speaking a language he does not know, but he does know that it has been given to him in order to praise God. The gift is for his own upbuilding. As someone speaks or sings in tongues, he surrenders his tongue and his whole self to God, letting go of his own words and ideas. Tongues is a gift for praise and in this praise the Life of God takes deeper root. It seems to me that the gift of tongues is best illuminated by St Paul's words in chapter 8 of the letter to the Romans: 'When we cannot find words to pray, the Spirit himself intercedes for us with sighs too deep for words'. The Spirit prays the primordial prayer of Christ, and so unites the Christian with Christ, and with the Father. In prayer groups, when people pray and sing in tongues together, the atmosphere of praise is both strong and uplifting.

The gift of healing also has the purpose of drawing people into deeper relationship with the Father through the Son. The prayer of people today is often the prayer of people who are lonely, sick or unhappy. Those who have the gift of healing and exercise a ministry of healing do so in the conviction that the Church's function is to carry on Christ's ministry for the transformation of individuals and of society. Francis McNutt, one of the most popular writers on healing, expresses its importance as follows:

> Jesus was typically Hebrew in his view of man: he did not divide man into body and soul, but saw him as a whole person. He came to save persons, not just souls. He came to help the suffering in whatever way they were suffering. Sickness of the body was part of the Kingdom of Satan he had come to destroy.[12]

The ministry of healing is a ministry to the whole person: it is prayer for that total liberation and transformation of the person that is according to the mind of God.

Another feature of charismatic renewal is prayer groups and, indeed, new forms of Christian community. Especially in America, there have grown up various charismatic covenanting communities where people commit themselves to one another and seek, as a community, to discover God's gift and his call; to receive his blessings and to know his will.

Conclusion

A general survey of contemporary Christian spirituality is beyond the scope of this short essay. All I have tried to do is to identify some of the features of contemporary Christian spirituality that bear the mark of our own times. These developments have not occurred in isolation. They have both stimulated and been stimulated by developments within systematic theology, especially ecclesiology and the theology of grace. The openness of Catholic spirituality to the insights of other churches and communions must be seen against the background of the Second Vatican Council's Decree on Ecumenism. Similarly openness to non-Christian religions against the background of the Decree on Relations with non-Christian Religions.

Contemporary spiritual writing may best be judged in two ways. First of all by its consistency with the Christian tradition, the tradition with which these essays have been concerned. Secondly, by its power to speak to people today: to call them from despair to hope, from darkness to light, from preoccupation with themselves, to an openness to divine love.

Notes and references

Introduction

1. Bismarck is credited with the callous remark that only a fool learns by his experience whereas a wise man learns by other people's.
2. See the text of Conrad of Marburg for the Office of Readings of *The Divine Office* on the Feast of St Elizabeth of Hungary, 17 November.
3. *Mémoires du duc de Saint-Simon*, ed. Chéruel and Regnier (Paris: Hachette, 1908 edition), vol. XII, p. 184.
4. *The Spiritual Letters of Dom John Chapman*, ed. Dom Roger Hudleston (London: Sheed and Ward, 1954 edition), p. 109 and see von Hügel's use of this dictum, p. 129 below. Cf. 'I hold to my view that we ought to try to do what we can, and not what we can't. Also that we should stick to the spiritual books which suit us, not to those which give us no help', p. 57.
5. See K.A. Wall, article 'Direction, Spiritual' in *New Catholic Encyclopedia* (Washington, Catholic University of America, 1966), vol. IV, pp. 888-90.
6. *'Eh, Monsieur le Curé, j'avise le Bon Dieu et il m'avise'*. Aviser in 'High' French means to perceive, to catch a glimpse of; that is the meaning which the *Curé* indicated when he told the story: *'il regardait le Bon Dieu, et le Bon Dieu le regardait … Tout est là'*. But the meaning of *aveuser* in patois is slightly different. It refers to the way a peasant looks at land or at cattle so as to appreciate their true worth; he appraises them knowing what is within; he can see them as from the inside; he can see them through and through. I have tried to render that in my transation. See A. Dupleix, *Comme insiste l'amour: présence du Curé d'Ars* (Paris: Nouvelle Cité, 1986), p. 135; *Jean Marie Baptiste Vianney Curé d'Ars: Pensées*, edited by B. Nodet (Tournai: Desclée de Brouwer), p. 86: B. Nodet, 'Pris du peuple pour le peuple', *Esprit Saint* 140 (1986), p. 11.

Chapter 2: The Prayer of Jesus

1. J. Jeremias, *New Testament Theology* (London: SCM, 1971), pp. 76-121.
2. N. Perrin, *Rediscovering the Teaching of Jesus* (London: SCM, 1962), pp. 146-8.
3. J. Jeremias, *The Parables of Jesus* (London: SCM, 1963 edition), pp. 139-144.
4. *Ibid*. p. 144.
5. C.S. Lewis, *The Great Divorce: A Dream* (London: Geoffrey Bles, 1946), pp. 31-2.
6. N. Perrin, *Rediscovering the Teaching of Jesus*, p. 149.

Chapter 3: The spirituality of the Desert Fathers

1. *The Sayings of the Desert Fathers*, tr. Benedicta Ward (London: Mowbrays, 1981), no. 39, p. 93.
2. *Ibid.*, no. 111, p. 183.
3. *Ibid.*, no. 3, p. 139.
4. From the Greek verb *anachoreo* meaning *to retire, to withdraw*.
5. *The Sayings of the Desert Fathers*, no. 1, p. 212.
6. Athanasius' *Life of Anthony*, tr. Robert Gregg (London: SPCK, 1950), no. 10, p.39; no. 521, p. 70.
7. *The Sayings of the Desert Fathers*, no. 7, p. 71.
8. *Ibid.*, no. 2, p. 227.
9. *Ibid.*, no. 10, p. 28.
10. *Ibid.*, no. 2, p. 138.

11. A *lavra* is a cluster of cells or caves in which a small community of monks would live, usually under a much respected Abba. The name derives from the Greek word *laura*, meaning an alley or lane in a city, which was first applied to the connecting passages between the caves, then to the whole community.
12. *The Life of Pachomius* (Vita Prima), ed. by Halkin in *Subsidia Hagiographica 19* (Brussels, 1932), no. 27; quoted in D. Chitty, *The Desert A City* (London: Mowbrays, 1977), p. 23.
13. Athanasius' *Life of Anthony*, no. 67, p. 81.

Suggested Further Reading

Sayings of the Desert Fathers, trs. Benedicta Ward (London: Mowbrays, 1981)
Athanasius' *Life of Anthony* (London: SPCK, 1980).
The Wisdom of the Desert: Sayings from the Desert Fathers of the Fourth Century, tr. Thomas Merton (London: Hollis and Carter, 1961).
Henri Nouwen, *Way of the Heart* (London: Darton, Longman and Todd, 1981).

Chapter 4: Three medieval English mystics

1. *The Cloud of Unknowing*, ed. William Johnston (New York: Doubleday, 1973), pp. 43-44.
2. *Ibid*. ch. 43, p. 103.
3. *The Epistle of Privy Counsel*, tr. Clifton Wolters (London: Penguin Books, 1978), ch. 7, p. 181.
4. *The Cloud of Unknowing*, ed. James Walsh SJ (London: SPCK, 1981) ch. 8, p. 138.
5. Walter Hilton, *The Stairway of Perfection*, tr. M.L. Del Mastro (New York: Doubleday, 1979) ch. 24, p. 251. This similarity between Hilton and the author of the Cloud is pointed out by Conrad Pepler OP on p. 267 of his *The English Religious Heritage* (London: Blackfriars, 1958).
6. *The Cloud of Unknowing*, tr. Clifton Wolters (London: Penguin Books, 1961), ch. 7, p. 69.
7. *The Cloud of Unknowing*, ed. J. Walsh, ch. 37, p. 193.
8. Julian of Norwich, *Revelations of Divine Love*, ed. C. Wolters (London: Penguin Books, 1976) ch. 66, p. 181.
9. Julian of Norwich, *Showings*, tr. E. Colledge OSA and J. Walsh SJ (New York: Paulist Press, 1978) ch. 16, Short Text, p. 153.
10. *Ibid*. ch. 5, Long Text, p. 183.
11. *Ibid*. ch. 27, p. 225.
12. *Ibid*. ch. 14, Short Text, p. 148.
13. *Ibid*. ch. 49, Long Text, p. 264.
14. *Ibid*. ch. 86, Long Text, p. 342.
15. Walter Hilton, *The Stairway of Perfection*, tr. M.L. Del Mastro, (New York: Doubleday, 1979) Bk. II, ch. 10, p. 210.
16. *Ibid*. Bk II, ch. 28, p. 266.
17. *Ibid*. Bk I, ch. 25, p. 94.
18. *Ibid*. Bk I, ch. 27, p. 96.
19. *Ibid*. Bk I, ch. 32, p. 101.
20. *Ibid*. Bk II, ch. 24, p. 250.
21. *Ibid*. Bk II, ch. 24, p. 251.
22. *Ibid*. Bk II, ch. 25, p. 253.
23. *Ibid*. Bk II, ch. 34, p. 287.

Suggested further reading

I have not followed the text of any one edition but quote from various editions and modern translations.

The following are the most easily available editions:

The Cloud of Unknowing and Other Works, tr. C. Wolters (London: Penguin Books, 1978).

The Cloud of Unknowing and The Book of Privy Counselling, edited and introduced by W. Johnston (New York: Image Books, 1973). Johnston's introduction is very useful.

The Cloud of Unknowing, edited and introduced by J. Walsh, SJ. Preface by Simon Tugwell, OP (London: SPCK, 1981). An extensive scholarly introduction. This is a large format paperback, very pleasing to read.

Julian of Norwich, *Revelations of Divine Love*, translated and introduced by C. Wolters (London: Penguin, 1973).

Julian of Norwich, *Showings*, translated and introduced by E. Colledge, OSA and J. Walsh, SJ. Preface by J. Leclercq, OSB (Paulist/SPCK, 1978). This contains both the short and long versions.

Julian of Norwich, *Revelations of Divine Love*, translated and introduced by C. Wolters (London: Penguin, 1966).

Walter Hilton, *The Stairway of Perfection*, translated with an excellent introduction by M.L. Del Mastro (New York: Doubleday, Image Books, 1979). This is the only full edition currently available. The introduction is very helpful.

Walter Hilton, *The Scale of Perfection*, abridged and presented by Illtyd Trethowan (London: Chapman, 1975). This is a radical abridgment, but useful to get a 'taste' for Hilton.

The best single book on the English Mystics that I know is that of Conrad Pepler, OP's, *The English Religious Heritage* (London: Blackfriars, 1958). Sadly now out of print, it can still be found in good libraries. With wonderful modesty and integrity it whets the reader's appetite for the original authors and directs one to their writings. Anyone familiar with the book will be aware of its influence on this essay.

Chapter 5: The *Imitation of Christ*

1. For a statement of the present consensus on the authorship of the *Imitation* see the article 'Imitation of Christ' by W.J. Alberts in *New Catholic Encyclopedia*, vol. VII, pp. 375-6.
2. Eckhart (c. 1260-1327 or 1328), generally known as Meister Eckhart because he was a Master of Theology of Paris University, taught a form of spirituality from an intellectualist interpretation of the theology of St Thomas Aquinas; see the article 'Eckhart, Meister' by F. Vandenbroucke in *New Catholic Encyclopedia*, vol. V, pp. 39-40.
3. *Summa Theologica* IIa IIae, a. 188, art. 5.

Chapter 6: Without a shadow of compromise: the unlovable mystic, John of the Cross

1. E. Allison Peers, *St John of the Cross* (London: Faber, 1932), p. 13.
2. *Ibid.*, p. 14.
3. See G. Brenan, *St John of the Cross* (Cambridge: CUP, 1973), pp. 16-18 for an example of such asceticism as revealed in the life of a certain Dōna Catalina de Cordova.
4. *Ibid.*, p. 15.
5. *Ibid.*, p. 23.

6. *Ibid.*, p. 47.
7. *The Spiritual Letters of Dom John Chapman*, ed. Dom Roger Hudleston (London: Sheed and Ward, 1954 edition), p. 269.
8. See J.C. Nieto, *Mystic Rebel Saint: A Study of St John of the Cross* (Geneva: Droz, 1979), pp. 21-7 for a discussion of the possible influences on John of the Cross, including Pseudo-Dionysius the Areopagite.
9. Ignatius Loyola, *The Spiritual Exercises*; the First Exercise for the First Week.
10. See for example St Bernard's Sermon 43 on the *Song of Songs*.
11. K.H.H. Wojtyla, *Faith according to John of the Cross*, tr. Jordan Aumann (San Francisco: Ignatius Press, 1981), p. 238. A fuller but concise summary of John's teaching considered in the next section of this study can be found in R. Williams, *The Wound of Knowledge* (London: Darton, Longman and Todd, 1979), pp. 159-179.
12. K.H.H. Wojtyla, *op.cit.*, p. 113.
13. *Counsels and Light and Love* (London: Burns and Oates, 1953, 1977) p. 52.
14. A. Damaso, *La Poesia de San Juan de la Cruz* (Madrid: Consejo superior de Investigaciones Cientificas, 1942).
15. John of the Cross, *The Living Flame of Love*, tr. David Lewis (London: Baker, 1919), p. xvi. The introduction takes the form of an essay by Cardinal Wiseman on John of the Cross.
16. F. Forresti, 'Le radici bibliche della Salita del Monte Carmelo di San Giovanni della Croce', *Carmelus* 28 (1981), pp. 226-55.
17. E. Allison Peers, *Spirit of Flame* (London: SCM, 1979 edition), p. 126.
18. T. Tyrrell, *Urgent Longings* (Whitinsville: Affirmation Books, 1980).

Chapter 7: St Francis de Sales

1. M. Muller, *St Francis de Sales* (London: Sheed and Ward, 1936), p. 70.
2. H.U. von Balthasar *The Glory of the Lord* (Edinburgh: T. & T. Clarke, 1982).
3. *Ibid.*, p. 92.
4. *St Francis de Sales: Selected Letters*, tr. E. Stopp (London: Faber, 1960), p. 20.
5. *Ibid.*, p. 51.
6. *Ibid.*, p. 64.
7. *Introduction to the Devout Life*, tr. M. Day (London: Burns and Oates, 1956), p. 139.
8. *Ibid.*, p. 185.
9. From St Vincent de Paul's testimony at the Paris Diocesan Enquiry of 1628 on the sanctity of St Francis de Sales; quoted in F. Trochu, *Saint François de Sales* (Lyons: Emmanuel Vitte, 1946), vol. II, pp. 631-2. Translation mine.

Suggested further reading

Works of St Francis de Sales

St Francis de Sales: Selected Letters, tr. Elisabeth Stopp (London: Faber, 1960).

Introduction to the Devout Life, tr. Michael Day, (London: Burns and Oates, 1956).

Treatise on the Love of God, tr. Henry Benedict Mackey (London: Burns and Oates, 1884).

Other works

Harold Burton, *The Life of St Francis de Sales* (London: Burns and Oates, 1952).

Michael de la Bédoyère, *François de Sales* (London: Collins, 1960).

Maurice Henry-Coüannier, *St Francis de Sales and His Friends*, tr. Veronica Morrow (London: Sceptre, 1964).

Michael Muller, *St Francis de Sales* (London: Sheed and Ward, 1936).

Elisabeth Stopp, *Madame de Chantal* (London: Faber, 1962).

Chapter 8: English recusant spirituality

1. J.M. Blom, *The Post-Tridentine English Primer* (Catholic Record Society, Monograph Series 3, 1982), p. 13.
2. *Ibid.* p. 112.
3. *Ibid.* p. 113.
4. John Gother (c. 1654-1704) was ordained priest at Lisbon in 1676 and returned to England in 1680. He wrote apologetic works to counter the anti-Catholic propaganda engendered by the Oates Plot. He later became chaplain at Warkworth Castle in Northamptonshire where he continued to write but now he was engaged in devotional rather than controversial works and few saw the light till after his death. They then appeared separately and in a collected edition of sixteen volumes of which five editions appeared before 1790, G. Anstruther, *The Seminary Priests* (Great Wakering: Mayhew-McCrimmon, 1976) vol. III, p. 83. See G. Every, 'John Gother with Laborious Christians 1680-1704', *Heythrop Journal* 23 (1982) pp. 30-45.
5. A. Wright, *The Counter-Reformation* (London: Weidenfeld and Nicolson, 1982), p. 268.
6. On Simon Verepaeus see J.M. Blom, *The Post-Tridentine English Primer* (Catholic Record Society, Monograph Series 3, 1982), ch. 6 'The history of the *Manual* from 1583-1800', especially pp. 112-115.
7. E. Duffy, 'Richard Challoner 1691-1781: A Memoir', in *Challoner and his Church: A Catholic Bishop in Georgian England*, ed. E. Duffy (London: Darton, Longman and Todd, 1981), p. 21.
8. E. Duffy, 'Richard Challoner and the Salesian Tradition', *The Clergy Review*, 66 (1981), p. 450.
9. R. Challoner, *Meditation for every day in the year* (London: 1934 edition), preface p. v.
10. *Ibid.*, preface, p. ix.
11. *Ibid.*, pp. 802-5, Meditation for 29 November.
12. R. Knox, *On Englishing the Bible* (London: Burns and Oates, 1949), p. 42.
13. F. Husenbeth, *History of Sedgley Park* (London: Richardson, 1856), p. 80.
14. *Ibid.*, p. 77-8.
15. *Ibid.*, p. 159.
16. *Ibid.*, p. 159.
17. *Oscott Jubilee Book 1888* (Oscott College Archives; I am grateful to the Rector of Oscott for permission to quote from these).
18. E. Duffy, 'Richard Challoner and the Salesian Tradition', *The Clergy Review* 66 (1981), p. 455. See also J.D. Crichton, 'Richard Challoner: Catechist and Spiritual Writer', *The Clergy Review* 66 (1981), pp. 269-75.

Chapter 9: Two Russian parish priests

1. *My Life in Christ . . . Extracts from the diary of the Most Reverend John Ilyitch Sergieff.* Tr. E.E. Goulaeff, (London: Cassell, 1897.)
2. *Spiritual Counsels of Father John of Kronstadt.* Select Passages from *My Life in Christ* edited and introduced by W. Jardine Grisbrooke (London: James Clarke, 1967; Cambridge and Crestwood, New York: James Clarke and St Vladimir's Seminary Press, 1981).
3. *The Diary of a Russian Priest* by Alexander Elchaninov, Tr. Helen Iswolsky; English edition prepared by Kallistos Timothy Ware. With an introduction by

Notes and references

Tamara Elchaninov, and a foreword by Dimitri Obolensky (London: Faber & Faber, 1967).
4. *A Treasury of Russian Spirituality*, compiled and edited by G.P. Fedotov (London: Sheed & Ward, 1950, 1952; Belmont, Massachusetts: Nordland Publishing). This quotation from p. 347, using the edition of 1952.
5. *Spiritual Counsels of Father John of Kronstadt*,
6. *Ibid.*, p. xvii.
7. *A Treasury of Russian Spirituality*, p. 348.
8. John Drury, *Angels and Dirt: An Enquiry into Theology and Prayer* (London: Darton, Longman & Todd, 1972), pp. 61, 62-3.
9. *The Diary of a Russian Priest*, p. 120.
10. *Ibid.*, p. 13.
11. *Ibid.*, p. 12.
12. *Ibid.*, p. 13.
13. *Ibid.*, p. 18.
14. *Ibid.*, p. 23.
15. *Ibid.*, pp. 22-23.
16. *A Treasury of Russian Spirituality*, p. 417.
17. *Ibid.*, p. 419.
18. *Ibid.*, p. 419.
19. *The Diary of a Russian Priest.*, pp. 20-21.

Chapter 10: The spirituality of the English Catholic modernists

1. For an introduction to the whole field of modernist research a good starting point is T.M. Loome, *Liberal Catholicism, Reform Catholics, Modernism: a Contribution to a New Orientation in Modernist Research* (Mainz: Grunewald, 1979). Most of the issues, personalities involved and relevant bibliographical material are indicated there. See also G. Daly, *Transcendence and Immanence: a Study in Catholic Modernism and Integralism* (Oxford: Clarendon Press, 1980) for a discussion of the theological questions raised by modernists.
2. Daly, *Transcendence and Immanence*, p. 19, see also J.J. Kelly, 'On the fringe of the Modernist Crisis: the correspondence of Baron Friedrich von Hügel and Abbot Cuthbert Butler', *Downside Review* 97 (1977), p. 275. Kelly's discussion of the fact that certain Catholic scholars felt the need to disengage from controversial areas of study is illuminating for understanding the intellectual background to the Modernist crisis in England. Loome has drawn attention to Edmund Bishop in this particular process, *Liberal Catholicism*, pp. 59ff, 425.
3. Tyrrell became even more convinced of this after staying at Richmond, see letter to Brémond, 4 August 1901, cited in G. Schultenover, *George Tyrrell: In Search of Catholicism* (Shepherdstown, 1981), p. 170. Peter Doyle's examination of seminary life and study is informative background, 'The Education and Training of Roman Catholic Priests in Nineteenth-Century England', *Journal of Ecclesiastical History* 35 (1984), pp. 208-19.
4. *The Faith of Millions*, first series (London: Longmans Green, 1901), p. v.
5. All these 'isms' were included in his final fierce attack on scholasticism: *Medievalism: A Reply to Cardinal Mercier* (London: Longmans Green, 1908).
6. *Oil and Wine* (London: Longmans Green, 1907), p. viii.
7. A. Loisy, *Mémoires pour servir à l'histoire religieuse de notre temps*, vol. I (Paris: Emile Nourry, 1930-1), p. 210.
8. Maude Petre, *Alfred Loisy: His religious significance* (Cambridge: CUP, 1944), pp. 13. Following quotation, p. 9f.
9. Laurence F. Barmann, *Baron Friedrich von Hügel and the Modernist Crisis in England* (Cambridge: CUP, 1972), p. 138.

10. Von Hügel, *The Mystical Element of Religion: as studied in Saint Catherine of Genoa and Her Friends*, vol. I (London: Dent, 1923), preface p. xxxiii, both quotations.
11. Letter of von Hügel to Wilfrid Ward, 31 December 1900, cited by Barmann, *Baron Friedrich von Hügel and the Modernist Crisis in England*, p. 78.
12. Loisy, *Mémoires*, vol. II, p. 72.
13. Tyrrell, *Lex Orandi: or Prayer and Creed* (London: Longmans Green, 1903), p. viii, both quotations.
14. Ellen Leonard, *George Tyrrell and the Catholic Tradition* (London: Darton, Longman and Todd, 1982), p. 19.
15. Tyrrell to Maude Petre, 2 June 1903; British Library, Add. Mss. 52367, 98B.
16. Daly, *Transcendence and Immanence*, p. 119.
17. Maude Petre, *Alfred Loisy*, pp. 33f. Loisy himself thought of von Hügel's God as the 'Grand Individu' and his insistence on transcendence 'un cauchemar angoissant', *Mémoires*, vol. III, p. 24.
18. Von Hügel, 'Father Tyrrell: Some memorials of the Last Twelve Years of His Life', *Hibbert Journal* 17 (1910) pp. 233-252.
19. Letter of von Hügel to Tyrrell, 14 May 1907, in *Baron Friedrich von Hügel: Selected Letters 1896-1924*, ed. B. Holland (London: Dent, 1928), p. 139. Immanence became for von Hügel the 'counter tyranny', M. de la Bédoyère, *The Life of Baron von Hügel* (London: Dent, 1951), p. 247.
20. Letter of von Hügel to Mrs Holiday, 10 January 1911; published by Duncan Macpherson, 'Von Hügel on George Tyrrell', *The Month* 231 (1971), p. 179.
21. Von Hügel, *The German Soul in its Attitude Towards Ethics and Christianity, The State of War; Two Studies* (London: Dent, 1916), p. 115.
22. See von Hügel 'On the Place and Function, within Religion, of the Body, of History, and of Institutions' in *Essays and Addresses on the Philosophy of Religion*, second series (London: Dent, 1926), pp. 59-87.
23. Von Hügel, *Essays and Addresses*, second series, p. 246.
24. Von Hügel, 'Experience and Transcendence', *Dublin Review* 138 (1906), p. 362.
25. *Ibid.*, p. 368.
26. P. Sherry, 'Von Hügel: Philosophy and Spirituality', *Religious Studies* 17 (1981), p. 7.
27. Tyrrell, 'Mysteries as a Necessity of Life' in *Through Scylla and Charybdis: or The Old Theology and the New* (London: Longmans Green, 1907), p. 163.
28. Tyrrell, *External Religion: Its Use and Abuse* (London: 1899), p. 119.
29. Maurice Blondel, 'Lettre sur les éxigences de la pensée contemporaine', in *Les Premiers écrits de Maurice Blondel*, vol II (Paris: Presses universitaries de France, 1956), p. 9.
30. Tyrrell, *Another Handful of Myrrh: Devotional Conference* (London: CTS, 1905), p. 9.
31. Tyrrell, *Nova et Vetera: Informal Meditations for Times of Spiritual Dryness* (London: Longmans Green, 1897), p. 185.
32. Letter of 29 June 1902 to V.; *Autobiography and Life of George Tyrrell*, vol. II (London: Edward Arnold, 1912), p. 14.
33. 'Revelation as Experience: An Unpublished Lecture of George Tyrrell', edited with notes on historical introduction by T.M. Loome, *Heythrop Journal* 12 (1971), pp. 117-49. All quotations in this paragraph are from this paper.
34. On Tyrrell's use of Arnold, see N. Sagorsky, *Between Two Worlds: George Tyrrell's Relationship to the Thought of Matthew Arnold* (Cambridge: CUP, 1963), ch. 7.
35. Daly, *Transcendence and Immanence*, p. 39.
36. David G. Schultenover, *George Tyrrell: In Search of Catholicism* (Shepherdstown: 1981), p. 218.
37. Tyrrell, *Lex Orandi*, p. xxv.
38. *Ibid.*, p. xxiv.
39. *Ibid.*, p. xxi.

Notes and references

40. Tyrrell, *Christianity at the Crossroads* (London: Longmans Green, 1963 edition), p. 176.
41. Maude Petre, *Where Saints Have Trod: Some Studies in Asceticism* (London, CTS, 1903); *The Temperament of Doubt* (London: CTS, 1903); *Devotional Essays* (London: CTS, 1904). Only part of *The Soul's Orbit or Man's Journey to God* (London: Longmans Green, 1904) was originally hers. On Maude Petre, see Clyde F. Crews, *English Catholic Modernism: Maude Petre's Way of Faith* (Notre Dame MSA, 1984) and Charles J. Healey SJ, 'Maude Petre: Her Life and Significance', *Recusant History* 15 (1979), pp. 23-42.
42. Maude Petre, *Where Saints Have Trod*, p. 18.
43. Maude Petre, *My Way of Faith* (London: Dent, 1937), p. 203.
44. Letter of 15 September 1921 in M. de la Bédoyère, *The Life of Baron von Hügel*, p. 337.
45. Von Hügel, *Mystical Element of Religion*, vol. I, p. 53.
46. Daly, *Transcendence and Immanence*, p. 131.
47. Von Hügel, *Essays and Addresses*, p. 185.
48. *Ibid.*, pp. 144-241.
49. Von Hügel, *Mystical Element of Religion*, vol. II, p. 287.
50. P. Sherry, 'Von Hügel: Philosophy and Spirituality', *Religious Studies* 17 (1981), p. 4.
51. Tyrrell 'What is Mysticism?' in *The Faith of Millions*, vol. I, pp. 253-72; see also *The True and False Mysticism*, pp. 273-344 from late 1899.
52. Tyrrell, *The Faith of Millions*, vol. I, p. 261.
53. *George Tyrrell's Letters* (London: Fisher and Unwin, 1920), p. 38; next quotation p. 53.
54. Tyrrell, *The Faith of Millions*, vol I, p. 271. Von Hügel's position on this question is close to that of Tyrrell. Next quotation from Hügel, p. 84.
55. William Johnston, *The Mirror Mind: Spirituality and Transformation* (London: Collins, 1981), p. 85.
56. L.V. Lester-Garland, *The Religious Philosophy of Baron Friedrich von Hügel* (London: Dent, 1933), p. 14.
57. Maisie Ward, *The Wilfrid Wards and the transition* (London: Sheed and Ward, 1934), p. 300.
58. Letter of 7 December 1908 in M.C. Petre, *Von Hügel and Tyrrell: The story of a friendship* (London: Dent, 1937), pp. 183-4.
59. Maude Petre, *Modernism: Its Failures and Its Fruits* (London: T.T. and E.C. Jack, 1918), p. 56.
60. Von Hügel, *Mystical Element of Religion*, vol. II, p. 266.
61. Quoted by Maisie Ward, *The Wilfrid Wards and the Transition*, p. 301.
62. *George Tyrrell's Letters*, p. 15.
63. Von Hügel, 'Experience and Transcendence', *Dublin Review* 138 (1908), p. 357-99.
64. *Letters from Baron von Hügel to a Niece* (London: Dent, 1928), p. xxi.
65. *Baron Friedrich von Hügel: Selected Letters 1896-1924*, ed. B. Holland (London: Dent, 1927), p. 348.
66. *Letters from Baron von Hügel to a Niece*, p. 3.
67. Von Hügel, *Essays and Addresses*, second series, pp. 217-42; all quotations are from these two addresses. For von Hügel on suffering see also *Selected Letters*, p. 227.
68. Tyrrell, *The Faith of Millions*, vol. I, p. 278; the next five quotations pp. 279, 280, 283, 284.
69. See 'The Relation of Theology to Devotion' in *The Faith of Millions*, vol. I, pp. 228-52.
70. *Ibid.*, p. 326.
71. Tyrrell, *Oil and Wine*, p. 258.

72. *George Tyrrell's Letters*, p. 147.
73. Eckhart, Sermon 'Qui audit me'; see R.B. Blakney, *Meister Eckhart: A Modern Translation* (New York: Harper Torchbooks, 1941), p. 204.
74. *George Tyrrell's Letters*, p. 149.
75. Tyrrell, *Lex Credendi: A Sequel to Lex Orandi* (London: Longmans Green, 1906), p. 135 and the next quotation.
76. *Ibid.*, p. 245.
77. Von Hügel, 'Fénelon's "Spiritual Letters" ', *The Tablet* 83, no. 2821, 2 June 1894, pp. 587-8. See also his reference to his debt to Père Grou in 'The Spiritual Writings of Père Grou, SJ', *The Tablet* 74, nos. 2589-90, 21-28 December 1889, pp. 990-1, 1029-31.
78. Von Hügel, *Letters to a Niece*, pp. 139-40.
79. *Ibid.*, p. xxiii.
80. M. Nédoncelle, *Baron Friedrich von Hügel: A Study of His Life and Thought* (London: Longmans Green, 1937), p. 169. See Also Joseph P. Whelan, *The Spirituality of Friedrich von Hügel* (London: Collins, 1971), p. 141.
81. J.J. Heaney, 'The Enigma of the Later von Hügel', *Heythrop Journal* 6 (1965), p. 157.
82. *The Letters of Evelyn Underhill*, ed. C. Williams (London: Longmans Green, 1951), p. 20.
83. Letter of Tyrrell to André Raffalovich, 16 June 1903; quoted by G. Daly, 'Some Reflections on the Character of George Tyrrell', *Heythrop Journal* 10 (1969), p. 263; and *Autobiography and Life of George Tyrrell*, vol. II, p. 2.
84. Ronald Chapman, 'The Thought of George Tyrrell' in *Essays and Poems Presented to Lord David Cecil*, edited by W.W. Robson (London: Constable, 1970) p. 14.
85. R.G.F. Jenkins, 'Tyrrell's Dublin Days', *The Month* 228 (1969), p. 11.
86. *Autobiography and Life of George Tyrrell*, vol. II, p. 14.
87. T.M. Loome, 'Revelation as Experience: An Unpublished Lecture of George Tyrrell', *Heythrop Journal* 12 (1971), p. 124. Maude Petre referred to him on one occasion as 'a restless, pugnacius being', *Baron von Hügel and Tyrrell: The Story of a Friendship*, p. 119.
88. On the important distinction between *pantheism* and *panentheism* see Von Hügel, *Essays and Addresses* , second series, p. 39 and p. 232, and *The Mystical Element of Religion*, vol. II, p. 325-35.
89. Tyrrell to von Hügel, 23 October, 1907, British Library, Add. Mss. 44930.72.
90. Hilda Graef, *Mystics of Our Times.* (London: Burns and Oates, 1962), ch. 4, 5, 8 or the first three of these.
91. Jordan Aumann, 'Christian Spirituality in the Catholic Tradition (London: Sheed and Ward, 1985), pp. 261-77.
92. Abbé de Tourville, *Letters of Direction: thoughts on the spiritual life*, ed. Evelyn Underhill (Oxford, Amiate Press 1984), p. 21. First published 1939, Mowbrays.

Chapter 11: A note on contemporary spirituality

1. Victor Codina, 'Learning to Pray Together with the Poor', *Concilium* 159 (1982), pp. 3-7.
2. Erich Neumann, *Mystical Man* Eranos Jahrbuch 30, 1968, referred to by Harvey D. Egan SJ., *What are they saying about mysticism?* (New York: Paulist Press, 1982).
3. H.A. Williams, *The True Wilderness* (London: Collins, 1983).
4. *Ibid.*, p. 31.
5. Hugh Lavery, 'A Meditation on the Fatherhood of God', *Clergy Review* 1972, pp. 676-679.
6. Thomas Merton, *Elected Silence* (London: Hollis and Carter), cf. also *The Seeds*

of Contemplation, (London: Catholic Book Club, 1956) and *The Ascent to Truth* (London: Hollis and Carter, 1951).

7. Quoted by Harvey D. Egan, *What are they saying about mysticism?*, p. 53.
8. Bede Griffiths, *Return to the Centre* (London: Collins, 1976).
9. William Johnstone, *The Inner Eye of Love, The Still Point: Reflections on Zen and Christian Mysticism, Christian Zen, Silent Music, The Mirror Mind: Spirituality and Transformation*, all published by Collins, London.
10. See *Silent Music*, ch. 8.
11. For a good introduction, see Simon Tugwell, *Did you receive the Spirit ?*, (London: Darton Longman and Todd, 1972).
12. Francis McNutt, *Healing* (Notre Dame, Indiana: Ave Maria Press, 1974), pp. 62-63.